JUBILEE RAMBLES

With East Yorkshire and Derwent Area
of the Ramblers' Association

edited by

Ann Holt

HUTTON PRESS
1988

Published by the Hutton Press Ltd.
130 Canada Drive, Cherry Burton, Beverley
East Yorkshire HU17 7SB

Printed and Bound by

Clifford Ward & Co. (Bridlington) Ltd.
55 West Street, Bridlington, East Yorkshire
YO15 3DZ

ISBN 0 907033 64 4

CONTENTS

ACKNOWLEDGEMENTS

The Editor wishes to acknowledge the assistance of the following in the preparation of this book:

K.R. Scurr, for drawing the maps.
Nonie McKiernan, for providing the line drawings.
Stuart Rennie, for the cover photograph
Roy Dresser, David Rubinstein and Ray Wallis for the inside photographs.

East Yorkshire and Derwent Area of the Ramblers' Association are most grateful to the Countryside Commission, Yorkshire and Humberside Regional Office, for generous financial assistance.

ABOUT THE CONTRIBUTORS

David Rubinstein was elected Area Secretary in 1966 and has served on its Committee in a variety of capacities. He was first elected to the RA's National Executive in 1967, and in 1987 completed a three-year term as RA Chairman.

Stuart Rennie became Footpath Secretary of the Driffield Group and a member of the Area Executive Committee in 1985; followed by Area footpath inspection Secretary in 1987.

Dennis Parker has been the Area Chairman for 15 years and devised the High Hunsley Circuit challenge walk for the Beverley Group. As a chartered surveyor he is keenly interested in the law relating to land.

Roy Dresser has been active in the area since 1971. He is currently the Area's Vice-Chairman, and has been secretary to the Hull and Holderness Group since its foundation in 1980.

Geoff Eastwood is a past Area Secretary and is currently Footpath Secretary. He is also a member of the RA's National Executive, is author of "Walking in East Yorkshire", and finds time to be a District Councillor on Beverley Borough Council.

Ray Wallis has been the Area's Assistant Footpath Secretary and Chairman of the Footpath Sub-Committee since 1984.

Sheila Smith has been Area Secretary for three years and before that was Minutes Secretary.

Betty Hood has been Secretary of the Ryedale Group since 1975 and for the last five years has been a member of the North York Moors National Park Committee.

Colin Coombes, a retired civil servant, has been a member of the York Group's Committee for four years and its Secretary for the past two.

Ann Holt, the editor, is a writer and researcher working on a variety of social and countryside topics. She is currently working on a book left unfinished by Tom Stephenson, former Secretary of the National RA, who died in 1987 at the age of 94.

Thornwick Bay

PREFACE

This booklet is a celebration - it celebrates the fiftieth birthday of the East Yorkshire and Derwent Area of the Ramblers' Assocation, and it celebrates our local countryside. We all hope that it will add to the enjoyment which both visitors and residents of our part of the world can have in the outdoors, by exploring its great variety of scenery in the best possible way - on foot. There is something here for everyone, experienced walkers, occasional walkers, loners, families, groups; we are lucky to have an area which offers so many different kinds of walking experience, wide plains, hidden valleys, rolling hills, long views in the clear eastern air and, unlike many areas with more glamorous claims to be walkers' country, the sea is never far away.

Having spent most of my working life with the Youth Hostels Association, I am always delighted to see more and more people, whole new generations, discovering the excitement and pleasures of walking in the open air. I am also aware of the amount of work which goes on behind the scenes to make it possible. The walks described here are all signed by the individual authors because we deliberately set out to give an idea of the enthusiasms and approaches to the outdoors which exist among RA members in a way in which no impersonal style of writing and presentation could achieve. And because the contributors are mostly RA activists something of the hours of work involved in making sure the path network is available for other people who want to walk comes through in what they write.

This is particularly acute in an area like ours which is almost all intensively farmed. There have been times when there seemed to be very little common ground indeed between the farming community and ramblers. Happily, there are signs of change. With the growing importance of leisure and tourism as an economic resource and as it becomes more and more apparent that the existing levels of European Community subsidy for agriculture cannot be maintained, perhaps the economic climate is more conducive to a move towards détente.

One welcome contribution to this is the *Ploughing and rights of way* code recently published jointly by the Countryside Commission and the Ministry of Agriculture, Fisheries and Food, and endorsed by, among others, both the National Farmers' Union and the Ramblers' Association. It makes the point that public rights of way are, in legal terms, highways with the same protection as metalled roads. Footpaths which run across fields can legally be ploughed, but should be

7

restored within two weeks. Ploughed-out footpaths have been all too common in East Yorkshire and Derwent Area. We all hope that this coming together by the Countryside Commission and MAFF will mark the beginning of a new era of respect for the ancient right of passage on the Queen's highway, even when that highway is a simple footpath across a field.

Gerald McGuire,
President, East Yorkshire and Derwent Area
Ramblers' Association.
February 1988

INFORMATION

The Ramblers' Association

The Ramblers' Association has three levels of organisation. At the grass roots level are the Groups, and the next tier is made up of Areas, which send delegates to the yearly National Council. At National Council a national Executive Committee is elected. The Association has a national office in London, and is a registered charity with three main aims:

> — to protect the network of footpaths and other rights of
>   way, and to increase access to open country
>
> — to defend outstanding landscapes
>
> — to encourage people to walk in the countryside.

It carries out these aims at national level through the employment of staff to run national campaigns, lobby MPs and generally to co-ordinate the Association's work. At local level, we have voluntary workers throughout the Areas and Groups who tackle the many footpath problems by reporting them to highway authorities and by carrying out necessary practical work, such as stile-building and waymarking. Areas and Groups also organise their own programmes of rambles and social events.

The Ramblers' Association national office address is

> The Ramblers' Association
> 1/5 Wandsworth Road,
> London SW8 2XX.

The local contact for the East Yorkshire and Derwent Area is

> Sheila M. Smith
> 65 Ormonde Avenue,
> Beresford Avenue,
> Beverley High Road,
> Hull HU6 7LT.

USING THIS BOOK

Maps

We hope that you will enjoy the walks in this book. Each walk has a sketch map, but you are strongly recommended to use the relevant Ordnance Survey map in conjunction with it and the text. For this reason sheet numbers and Grid References have been included in each walk.

Public Transport

Details of public transport are included in all walks where it exists at the time of writing. However, if you are intending to use buses or trains it is essential to check before you start as timetables are subject to change. This is especially the case in the winter and on Sundays when many services are less frequent or non-existent, particularly near the coast.

Trains:

Bridlington 0262 672056
Hull 0482 26033
York 0904 642155

Buses:

Connor and Graham
Easington 0964 650236

East Yorkshire Motor Services

Hull 0482 27146
Beverley 0482 881213
Bridlington 0262 673142
Driffield 0377 42133
Scarborough 0723 754643

Reliance Motor Services

York 0904 768262

Reynard Pullman Coaches

York 0904 22992

West Yorkshire Road Car Co.

Scarborough 0723 375463

Youth Hostels

Beverley 0482 881751
Malton 0653 692077
Thixendale 0377 88238
York 0904 653147

Footpath Problems

If you come across any footpath problems in our area, by all means let us know. But why not write to the County Council as well?

Humberside

Director of Technical Services
Humberside County Council
County Hall
Beverley HU17 9BA

North Yorkshire

County Engineer and Surveyor
Highways and Transportation Department
North Yorkshire County Council
County Hall
Northallerton
N. Yorks DL7 8AH

INTRODUCTION

Why Walk?

If you have picked up this book because you have already dis-covered the joys of walking then the question will be superfluous. But maybe you are just glancing at it, wondering whether you should try a bit of this rambling people are always talking about. If you read on you will not get a dis-passionate account. No rambler is ever dis-passionate about walking. We find it a source of infinite interest, pleasure and satisfaction. Part of the reason why East Yorkshire and Derwent Area of the Ramblers' Association decided to compile this book is that we feel that, although rambling is already the most popular form of outdoor recreation, even more people should take it up and share our enthusiasm for the outdoors.

Perhaps the first point to make, in this health-conscious age, is that walking is very good for you. One of the hazards of writing about the history of rambling, which I do from time to time, is the large number of ramblers who live long lives and keep their faculties to the end. So there is always someone around who was at that crucial meeting in 1931, remembers exactly what was decided and why, and is perfectly able to write you a long letter telling you, in considerable detail, why your article is complete rubbish. On these occasions I find my gratitude is somewhat less than total, but my conviction that rambling brings long life and good health reinforced.

So if you want to keep your mind and body in full working order, you can't do better than develop the habit of walking. You don't have to be fit to start with and you can tailor the amount of effort you have to expend to what suits you. It is not the sort of violent exercise which gives office-workers heart attacks. Provided you are reasonably sensible you are highly unlikely to get injured. You can begin very young and it will be a long, long time before you become too infirm to enjoy walking at all.

Quite apart from the health argument, walking is a very compre-hensive form of recreation. It can be physically, aesthetically and intellectually satisfying. The exercise is pleasant in itself, you will see beautiful countryside and come across things and experiences which can send you off to follow up the most unlikely avenues of fact and fiction. It is recreation for all seasons (once you have the rambling bug it will take more than rain to keep you indoors), all places (plenty of opportunities in Britain and abroad), and all temperaments - you can walk alone to commune with your soul, with a congenial friend or two for companionship or with an organised group to improve your social life.

Rambling allows people to take what they need as individuals. If you want to test yourself to the limits, then rambling will give you the chance just as it will if what you want is to leave the stress behind. On the other hand, if you want to see plants and birds, or just to delight the eye with the way a hillside curves down or a tree stands up against the sky, rambling will give you that opportunity too.

Finally, of all sports and recreations, rambling must be the most beginner-friendly. Provided you don't assume that you can do 30 miles over rough country before tea on your first outing, you can enjoy it from the start. You don't need to spend a lot of money before you know whether rambling is really for you or not. You can do if you want to - there is plenty of highly-priced outdoor chic in the sports shops. When you want to move on to the tougher stuff you will be well advised to do so properly equipped. But you can begin with any reasonably hardwearing and comfortable clothing and footwear, bearing in mind that the outdoors is prone to be colder, dirtier and wetter than the indoors and that pain in the feet will cast a blight on your psyche which the most ravishing view won't diminish.

But you don't have to invest in expensive boots for your first ramble. Trainers, thick socks and a waterproof will take you a long way provided the weather, distance and terrain are reasonable - which they usually are in East Riding and Derwent Area. After all, we have one of the lowest average rainfalls in the country, surprising though that may seem sometimes. If you are thinking of giving rambling a try, you would do well to start off with a few organised group rambles, where you won't have to take on the responsibility of route-finding right from the start. You will be very welcome to come out with any of the rambles organised by East Riding and Derwent Area of the RA.

Why Walk in East Riding and Derwent?

When we held our opening ceremony for the Wolds Way, the Area's only official Long Distance Footpath, we were joined by some friendly folk from the Sheffield Campaign for Access to Mountains and Moorlands. I asked one of them whether he had enjoyed the opening walk. He hesitated. 'Yes' he said 'very much - but it's a bit -

well - *arable* for us.' And he was quite right. If you are only happy walking on open country, across mountain and moorland, then the East Riding and Derwent Area is not for you. Not even a local patriot could say that it has the attractions of honey-pot areas like the Lake District or the Yorkshire Dales.

But I personally think we are too self effacing when it comes to describing our local landscape. Words like 'modest', 'domestic' and 'tamed' turn up far too often. It is certainly a lowland landscape, southern-looking in many ways, in spite of being north of the Trent, bounded by the Vale of York to the west, the plain of Holderness to the east, the Vale of Pickering to the North and the Humber estuary to the south. Our favourite walking country tends to be the Wolds, which occupy the centre of our region, and the Howardian Hills in the north-west corner of our area. Our 'high places' are in the Wolds which only occasionally exceed 600 feet above sea-level.

However, we all fall victim too easily to the chocolate box school of landscape appreciation. It just isn't the case that countryside needs to have either the nostalgic prettiness of the cottage with roses round the door, or the rugged grandeur of the Carneddau or Knoydart to be worth looking at or walking in. Landscape can be aesthetically pleasing in a vast variety of ways. If we look at the work of the great artists, who are, after all, the professionals when it comes to understanding what is interesting and pleasing to the eye, they have painted a lot of the sort of landscape which would never turn up on calendars if they hadn't painted it first. Flat country, of which we have quite a lot, is often thought boring. Constable painted a lot of flat country. The impressionists didn't have to head for the mountains to find inspiration; a few poplars were quite sufficient for them to create something which would nowadays raise millions in an art auction. To come up to our own time, many of the landscapes photographed by the current RA national president, Fay Godwin, are not 'pretty' scenery. They are so striking because they convey an understanding of a particular landscape as it is, its individual shapes, relationships and qualities.

What rambling offers is the chance to experience a landscape, whether urban or rural, with an intensity which merely looking at it will never give. The rambler walks into the landscape and becomes part of it. It is experienced with all the senses, touch, taste, smell and sound as well as sight. The walks in this book will give you an excellent introduction to the qualities of our landscape and I am sure your 'inward eye' will not be disappointed.

14

A Surprising Part of the World

As an incomer to this part of England I have never ceased to find it full of surprises; every new view is liable to open out onto something quite unexpected. Think of our two major seaside resorts, Bridlington and Scarborough. Raise your eyes for the moment from the amusement arcades of the front at Scarborough and you will see, towering above, a ruined castle as romantic as anything you are likely to see outside *The Count of Monte Cristo.* Allow yourself to be tempted away from the fleshpots of Bridlington to Bempton Cliffs and Flamborough Head and you will find one of the most dramatic stretches of coastline in the kingdom. Even the smaller seaside town of Hornsea, a prosaic enough place at first glance, turns out to have a prizewinning museum and a mere, sole survivor of many which once dotted the flat, wet plain of Holderness.

If you walk on the Wolds, just when you have become accustomed to the sensation of walking on a wide, airy plateau the landscape will suddenly drop away into a steep-sided, narrow valley. It looks for all the world as though some massive scythe has passed over a group of conical peaks, cutting them to the knee.

The ultimate surprise is Spurn Head, called 'Yorkshire's last fling' by Clegg of Clegg's People on a recent television programme. The Spurn peninsula reaches out into the Humber, a mighty estuary ringed with industry, polluted and dangerous to shipping; it can also be beautiful and mysterious while the long curved lines of the Humber Bridge which span it are another surprise. The longest single-span suspension bridge in the world, it has become a tourist attraction in its own right.

The buildings also show this capacity for springing surprises. In southern Holderness, two mighty churches, Hedon and Patrington, reach up towards the wide skies of this flat land. Their existence is explained by these towns having, at one time, been ports with creek carrying ships down to the Humber. Changes in the navigable channels of the estuary and land reclamation to the south have left them marooned among the fields. The great architectural glories of our Area are, of course, to be found in York and Beverley, both unmissable for the visitor, but too well established on the tourist map to need further trailing here. But lovers of church architecture should note, for example, that the basically Norman church of Garton on the Wolds has some magnificent Victorian wall-paintings and should not

15

miss the church at Howden, which is all the more picturesque through being partially ruined. Even Hull, that most down-to-earth of cities, has numerous quirky corners which will repay an exploration and the Town Docks Museum brings its long association with the sea to life.

But the area is also rich in small market towns, each with its own atmosphere. Malton, stone-built, is the most picturesque, but Driffield provides a pleasing ensemble of the brick buildings characteristic of most of the area, with a bustling High Street and peaceful canal head where a warehouse has been carefully restored for residential use. Pocklington is also a place for connoisseurs of small towns, keeping well up to East Yorkshire standards of unexpectedness by having a museum devoted to penny arcade machines where you can revel in the innocent naughtiness of another age.

There are many other places in this area which could be mentioned - other people would certainly have included other places and things to draw your attention to. But I hope this personal reflection on walking and the delights of East Yorkshire and Derwent Area will tempt residents and visitors to explore it more fully, especially on foot.

Ann Holt
Hull
February 1988

A BRIEF HISTORY OF OUR AREA

The East Riding Ramblers' Federation, our predecessor, was founded on a Friday evening in Mid-February 1938 at 'a very crowded meeting' of about 70 people held in the Church Institute, Albion Street, Hull. Six organisations were represented, and many individuals without club affiliation also attended. The *Hull Daily Mail* report suggested that about 2,000 East Riding ramblers were affected by the activities of the bodies represented at the meeting. Three leading figures emerged. Thomas Stainforth was a prominent and popular writer, naturalist and teacher, whose rambling articles published in the *Mail* under the penname of 'Roamer' in 1929 were reprinted in 1948 as *Rambles around Hull.* The meeting was chaired by Charles Henry Drewry, chairman of Beverley Ramblers' Club, and subsequently chairman of the federation until his death in 1946. (He was succeeded as chairman by Dennis Monson, who also attended the inaugural meeting, and who remained in post until 1961). Drewery was also a remarkable figure, 'always up in arms against attempts to take away from the public any right of way', an obituary notice commented. He was also a field naturalist, geologist, gardener, traveller and local historian*. The third, more shadowy, character, was G.N. Pickersgill, who took the initial minutes and remained secretary until 1953.

The meeting had two objects. One was to expose the 'deplorable state' of the footpath between Cottingham and Beverley, and to arrange a public walk over the path. Drewry suggested that such a walk would help to draw 'public attention to the scandal of the East Riding footpaths, this particular path being a typical example'. Well may local ramblers feel that time passes but nothing changes! The other object was achieved by Stainforth's successful motion that 'a federation of East Yorks rambling organisations and individual ramblers be established with the object of preserving and extending local footpaths and dealing with all matters affecting ramblers'. The federation was thus born, its name changing in 1949, consequent upon the adoption of a new national constitution, to the East Riding Area of the Ramblers' Association, and then to the present East

I am grateful to Geoff Drewery, present Membership Secretary of East Yorkshire and Derwent Area, for information about his near namesake.

A mass ramble to protest at the loss of access to Millington Pastures in 1965.
Photo by courtesy of Roy Dresser

Yorkshire and Derwent Area when local government was re-organised in 1974.

The history of our Area has four principal stages, which can be termed periods of initiation, expansion, transformation and consolidation. The new federation began its work with a will, though it was long overshadowed by the local rambling clubs; it was not, indeed, until nearly thirty years after its foundation that the Ramblers' Association itself instituted a rambles programme. Regular meetings were held in 1938 amd early 1939. As early as 1938 a canvas of prospective members was undertaken and the East Riding was divided among eight members for reports on the condition of footpaths. Other matters discussed included incivility on the part of certain publicans, selection of delegates to the National Council of the Ramblers' Association and the compilation of a catering list, all familiar items half a century later. As in Cottingham, a mass ramble was planned to combat a blocked footpath at Hedon, another tactic which has not lost favour with the decades.

With the coming of war in September 1939 the federation suspended its meetings and did not resume them until March 1946. Nor was progress rapid thereafter, judging from the infrequency with which meetings were held. But change and expansion were on the way. 1949 was notable not only for the new constitution but for the passing of the National Parks and Access to the Countryside Act, which for the first time instructed local authorities to create a system of 'definitive' rights of way for the rambler and horserider. As Pickersgill reported to his committee in June 1950, the act was 'of the utmost importance to ramblers...it was up to us to carry out a survey of footpaths in readiness for the draft maps to be produced by the Council within the next three years.'

Although the East Riding County Council failed lamentably to carry out its job, the work done by local ramblers was of great importance; no other undertaking in our history has been so exacting or so crucial. We now (June 1951) meet in the minute book for the first time the name of Alan Dalton, one of the leaders of the survey team. Alan served for many years as an Area officer, including a period as chairman, and remains an honoured member. In June 1953 Stuart Wise was elected treasurer, serving with distinction in that post (and for a period as secretary) for over fifteen years before moving to Edinburgh. At the same time Mike Hurst, who was also to put in many years of valuable service, joined the committee. If the state of the definitive map in the East Riding became a byword for inefficiency and neglect, the same could not be said of the hard and painstaking work of the voluntary footpath surveyors, to whom so much of the area's present (but still inadequate) network of footpaths and bridle-ways is owed. Another important figure made his first appearance in 1959, when Terence Kirby was elected Area auditor, a post which he still fills cheerfully and unassumingly, to the great benefit of the Area in general and (in recent years) successive sweating, non-accountant treasurers in particular.

After the work involved in putting in claims for the creation of the original 'draft' map of rights of way in 1953 much of the Area's energy went into pressing the East Riding County Council to go through the remaining stages of the definitive map procedure. Judging from the minute book and the voluminous though sporadically kept Area scrap books, the next significant event came with the election of Bruce Riddell as secretary at the AGM in April 1964. Bruce's term of office was brief but important in inaugurating the period of transformation of the Area. He it was with P.J. (Paddy) Boylan who organised in November 1965 a mass protest ramble over the loss to the public of Millington Pastures, the last traditional green 'lung' remaining from pre-enclosure days. Though the common land was ploughed up and fenced certain important and well-used public rights of way were saved. Even more important was the fact that for the first time the Area had staged a mass public event which drew widespread publicity and several hundred people. The departure of Bruce and Paddy in the later 1960s, one to Scotland, the other to Devon, was a severe blow to the Area.

The process of transformation, however, continued. The arrival in the Area of a number of individuals with unusually flexible working hours, time to devote to the affairs of the Ramblers' Association and access to modern methods of communication had a considerable impact on the Area's fortunes. But more was owed to social factors than to individuals. The increase in the standard of living, the leisure explosion and the increased membership of countryside organisat-ions in the later 1960s were all significant factors, as was the passing of the Countryside Act in 1968. More people wanted to walk the paths, and they became increasingly irritated by the active or passive opposition of farmers and the indolence of local authorities. The result (encouraged by the interest shown by certain individuals in influential positions) was that the local press, radio and television

Tom Stephenson, RA National Secretary, addressing a rally to press for the Wolds Way long distance footpath in 1968

were well disposed towards our aims and gratified by the amount of publicity which our activities generated. The close co-operation between the Area and the national body, and the inspiration and assistance of successive national secretaries, Tom Stephenson, Chris Hall and Alan Mattingly, who were always ready to provide support when most needed, was of immeasurable help to us.

I succeeded Bruce Riddell as Area secretary in 1966, remaining in office until 1972. I had the help and support of a willing committee, among whom (besides those already named) must be mentioned Ray Hodge, a painstaking Press Officer gifted with flair and an attractive personality. I was succeeded by Geoff Eastwood, who later swapped the secretary's hat for that of footpath secretary, a position which he still holds. It is Geoff more than any other single person who has succeeded in making the Ramblers' Association both respected and feared, and who by his persistent effort has saved many footpaths from disappearing from the public domain.

21

In 1968, when national long-distance footpaths were becoming popular, the Area put forward a plan for a seventy-mile Wolds Way across the East Riding from the Humber to the North Sea, where it met the established Cleveland Way. The volume of favourable publicity generated surprised and delighted us, but it needed an unremitting team effort before the Wolds Way was finally opened in 1982. Because of a row about the appropriate choice of the best person as official 'opener' two simultaneous inaugural ceremonies were held, ensuring more publicity than we could have hoped for from a single uncontentious occasion. Indeed, not since the opening of Tom Stephenson's Pennine Way in 1965 can the name of the Ramblers' Association have been heard so loudly in this context.

As was to be expected, the Wolds Way stimulated the creation of many 'unofficial' long-distance footpaths, which have been signpost-ed, waymarked and walked by large numbers of enthusiastic ramb-lers. These include Ray Wallis's Minster Way, Dennis Parker's High Hunsley Circuit, Alan Killick's Hull Countryway and Glen Hood's Beverley Twenty. All of them are the creation of members of the RA's East Yorkshire and Derwent committee, most of whom remain in post; it would be invidious to pick and choose between them, but one must mention the stability which Dennis Parker has given the Area in fifteen years as chairman and his willingness to shoulder the unglamorous jobs which nobody else wished to do.

The Ramblers' Association not only works to save footpaths but is a body concerned with natural beauty and amenity. Three successes in this field were a scheme for the creation of thirteen country parks under the terms of the Countryside Act, which achieved much publicity and which was realised in part; our effective opposition to drowning the famous daffodil valley in Farndale to build a reservoir and to ruining the Flamborough Heritage Coast by creating a yachting marina there early in the 1970s.

But it is the preservation and improvement of the footpath system which has always been the main source of inspiration to the Ramblers' Association and to our Area. One outstanding case was that of the path through Welton Dale, where leading Area officials were under an injunction in the High Court for a number of years in the 1960s and 1970s. Through a combination of hard work, audacity and good luck the case was eventually dropped and Welton Dale now forms an accepted part of the Wolds Way. Many footpath cases have been fought to the accompaniment of a lower level of controversy at public inquiries by Geoff Eastwood, Richard Kenchington (who enjoyed a meteoric career as Footpath Secretary in the 1970s before he too moved elsewhere) and other members; each case caused only limited ripples but helped to create a network of paths in an area no less cherished than others where the scenery is superficially more attractive.

The national press, including both the *Guardian* and the *Sunday Times*, have visited the Area and carried important features on the local footpath system. Roy Dresser has not let us forget the importance of maintaining footpaths in urban areas and the value of the country's least known rambling area, Holderness. The Area footpath committee, now nearly twenty years old, has helped to save many paths and insisted effectively that footpaths are an important resource which must not be mistreated by farmers and landowners or ignored by the highway authority. A special word of thanks is owed to Jack Bower, the Area's only Rambles Secretary, who has created and co-ordinated a programme of rambles for almost twenty years. Long may he remain in post!

As the Ramblers' Association has grown, a third tier has developed below the national and area organisations. This consists of local groups. As early as 1954 Tom Stephenson called for the creation of a York group; it was later established and led first by David Nunns and then Colin Coombes. It has been followed by others in Ryedale, where Betty and Colin Hood have carried the RA banner with distinction for many years, Driffield, Beverley and Hull. It owes much to the work of the groups that, late in 1985 when the national association celebrated its fiftieth birthday and fifty thousandth member, the Area first reached a four-figure membership.

The Ramblers' Association has grown and developed in East Yorkshire. It has never shunned controversy, and remains now as it has been for years past the most active amenity body in our district. We have faced problems, we have occasionally had rows and we have lost crucial members at inconvenient times. But the struggle continues, as is shown by our successful participation in the national Forbidden Britain days in 1986 and 1987, when we highlighted missing or mistreated paths in North Ferriby and the Driffield area. The enthusiasm of our latest active member, Stuart Rennie, has been particularly valuable in this context. Like others of the new counties, Humberside County Council is more concerned about public rights of way than its predecessor authority, and favoured social and

23

political factors have played their part in this process. But much of the credit is owed to a body of volunteers who have consistently refused to take no for an answer, and who are conscious of the fact that they speak not for themselves alone but for the ever-increasing numbers of people who seek access to the countryside.

As our second half century begins it is evident that the problems which we face were familiar to Tom Stainforth, Charles Drewry, G.N. Pickersgill and Dennis Monson. Complacency is also inhibited by the fact that we have only begun to recruit as members the second half of the number of ramblers represented at our inaugural meeting. There is always a potential for conflict when one body of people seeks to exercise their right to walk over land owned by others, as there is over threats to the integrity of unspoiled rural areas, but it is also the case that there is a greater sense of responsibility on the part of farmers and local authorities than in the past. East Yorkshire and Derwent ramblers, proud of their jubilee, move confidently into the future, in the knowledge that their workload is unlikely to decline but that their cause is just and supported by a growing weight of public opinion.

David Rubinstein

A CIRCULAR WALK VIA NORTH DALTON, FRIDAYTHORPE, HUGGATE AND WETWANG

Starting point: *North Dalton, Grid Reference 935522*

Distance: *21 miles (about 9 hours)*

Maps: *Landranger 1:50,000 Sheet 106*
               Pathfinder 1:25,000 Sheet 666

Transport: *East Yorkshire Motor Services Bridlington/York*
               bus

Refreshment: *all villages*

This 21 mile circular walk traverses typical Wolds countryside, with gently rolling hills in the east and the steeper slopes and dales of the high Wolds to the west. The route described starts from the village of North Dalton, which lies 6 miles south-west of Driffield on the B1246. All Saints' Church stands on a hill overlooking the pond and has a Norman south doorway, chancel arch and font. Food and accommodation may be obtained throughout the year at The Old School Tearooms, while the Star Inn offers home cooking and hand-pumped real ale. The village also has a post office with shop and off-licence.

Walk northwards from the Star Inn, cross the road and take the narrow road to the left of the war memorial. Turn left at the T-junction, and left again at the signpost just before the cemetery. The path follows Dikers Lane, a sunken track which is mentioned in late twelfth-century charters. After 300 yards the lane ends abruptly at the edge of an arable field. Turn left and walk along the field edge with a wire fence on your left. Turn right at the field corner, and follow the grassy track on the north side of the hedge westwards for $1\frac{1}{4}$ miles to a concrete road. This section of the route climbs steadily, with views over Holderness opening up to the south-east.

Turn left along the road and after 40 yards turn right at the signpost onto another concrete road. After 600 yards the road passes a dew pond on the left, so called because they are rarely dry and were believed to be replenished by the nightly condensation of dew. They were built around the time of enclosure to provide water for farm animals and are found all over the Wolds. Research has shown that

25

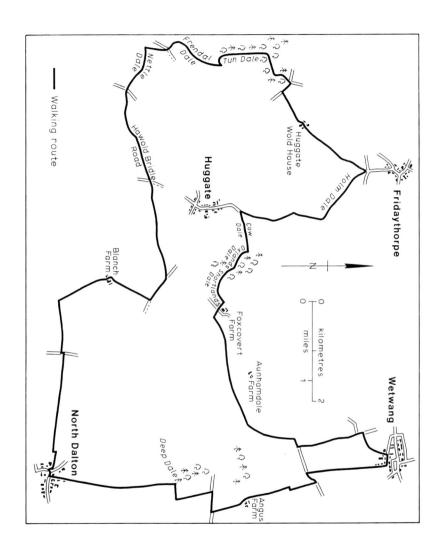

Walking route

Frendal Dale
Nettle Dale
Tun Dale
Huggate Wold House
Howold Bridle Road
Huggate
Holm Dale
Blanch Farm
Cow Dale
Harlands Dale
Sportans Dale
Foxcovert Farm
Aunhamdale Farm
Deep Dale
Angus Farm
North Dalton
Wetwang
Fridaythorpe

N

kilometres
0   1   2
miles
0   1   2

26

they are refilled not by dew but by rainwater, which is prevented from seeping into the chalk by a layer of puddled clay.

Continue westwards along the road, turning right at a footpath signpost along yet another concrete road which leads north to Blanch Farm. Follow the road through the farm to the North Dalton Huggate road (901542). Turn left and, after 600 yards, left again at a bridleway signpost, to follow the wide grass track known as the Hawold Bridleroad westwards along the south side of the fence. Cross the Huggate-Warter road after $1\frac{1}{4}$ miles and continue westwards, now with a large hedge on your right and a metal fence to left. The track climbs steadily, with fine views to the south, until it reaches a road at Cobdale Cottages (858537).

Cross straight over the road near the bridleway signpost, following the grass track on the south side of a hedge. There are large gaps in the hedge, through which you may be able to make out a group of low mounds in the field beyond. These are bronze age round barrows which, like many others on the Wolds, have been almost flattened by ploughing. Keep to the field edge, ignoring the track which goes off to the left, and cross a stile on the right 100 yards before entering a wood. Walk downhill to the west from the stile, passing through a clump of ash trees, and head for the right-hand side of a line of thorn trees. Follow these to the west until you reach a wire fence, with waymarks indicating a choice of routes, and a good view down Millington Dale. Turn right along the fence descending to the floor of Nettle Dale and climb the steep slope opposite. Keep to the wire fence, ignoring the Wolds Way signpost pointing right, and continue over the brow of the hill, over a stile, and down the slope to the floor of Millington Dale where another stile leads you onto the Huggate-Millington road.

Cross the road and continue northwards over a stile to the left of a bridleway signpost. The route ahead follows the route of a dry valley known here as Frendel Dale, becoming Tun Dale further north, and finally Greenwick Dale at the head of the valley. At a little over 200 feet deep, and with steeply sloping sides, it is a typical high wolds dry valley. Keep close to the fence up the valley bottom, crossing a fence by the gate or stile. The route makes a sharp left turn at a junction of dales (853555), shortly before bending round to the right to enter a Forestry Commission plantation by means of a handgate. Walk north along a track until a bridleway signpost indicates the way to the right at a junction of tracks. Immediately after turning right the track branches. Take the right fork, which climbs the hillside, bending left then right

A Typical Autumn scene on the Wolds between North Dalton and Huggate.
Photo by courtesy of Ray Wallis.

before emerging from the trees onto York Lane near a road junction.
Turn right towards Huggate, and after 275 yards turn left at the signpost along the drive to Huggate Wold House farm. The farm lies just over 700 feet above sea level, making it the highest point on the route. The view from the farm drive covers a vast area, eastwards to the coast and south-east over Beverley to Hull and the Humber estuary. Enter the farmyard at the south corner and cross diagonally to the north corner aiming for a yellow waymark. Turn right between farm buildings and leave the farm by the gate ahead. Follow the track north-east through gaps in two hedges to a third hedge where there is a fine view to the east across the head of the Hull valley. The track turns sharp left here, but the path continues in a generally northerly direction to rejoin the track 180 yards south-west of a gate and stile.

Turn right along the track, cross the stile and continue north-east, keeping close to the fence on your left until you reach a bridleway signpost near a fence and stile (874584). The village of Fridaythorpe lies 550 yards to the north along a green lane. Hand-pumped real ale and food may be obtained at the Cross Keys, and there is also a shop, post office, restaurant and cafe. All Saints' Church, restored in 1902, has a Norman tower, south doorway and chancel.

To continue the walk, head southwards from the bridleway sign-post, following a well-defined track down a narrow valley to Holm Dale. Turn left (south-east) and walk down the valley bottom until you reach a wire fence and gateway. Keep to the left of the gate and continue south-east with the fence on your right to another gate and stile. Turn right over the stile, and walk along the fence for a few yards before climbing the hillside to the left by a clear track noting the view up Horse Dale to the south-west. Pass through the handgate in the hedgerow at the top of the slope, until you reach the track leading to Northfield Farm. Turn right and walk down the hill until you reach a signpost and stile on the left leading down to Cow Dale (882559). The spire ahead, an unusual feature on the Wolds, is that of St. Mary's church, Huggate. The village has a post office and shop, and a well reputed to be 334 feet deep. The Wolds Inn offers food, accommodation and real ale.

Walk east down Cow Dale to a large solitary ash tree standing at the junction of three dales. Turn right (south), cross the stile and walk up Oxlands Dale, keeping close to the metal fence on the left. Continue up the valley passing through two metal gates and over a stile, and leave the fence to follow a well-defined track to the south-east up Shortlands Dale to a gate. Go through the gate and follow the track along the north side of a plantation before turning right at a junction of tracks to reach the Huggate-Wetwang road near Foxcovert Farm (902554).

Turn left, then right after 25 yards at a signpost and go through the gate. Walk along the field edge keeping the hedge on your right, with views to the north-east over Wetwang and Garton. After three fields cross the metalled road leading to Aunhamdale Farm and continue eastwards with the hedge still on your right. The hedge bends round from east to north-east until, eventually, you are walking due north. Turn right through a gap in the hedge at a waymaking post (929567), and follow the field edge east for a few yards then north for 375 yards to a signpost at the end of Green Lane. Turn right, then left after 200 yards through a gap in the hedge near a bridleway signpost. Follow the field edge northwards until you reach a track leading to the Huggate-Wetwang road.

Continue north along the road, turn right at the footpath signpost (928584) through the gateway, and walk eastwards along the field

Millington Dale, a typical Wolds dry valley. Photo by courtesy of Ray Wallis.

edge for 300 yards to a waymarking post. The path leaves the hedge, which turns sharply to the left here, and cuts across the field corner to the north-north-east to rejoin the hedge after 180 yards at another waymarking post. From here walk in a generally northerly direction, taking a line to the right of some farm buildings and head for a yellow signpost up the field. At the top of the field cross the stile onto Southfield Road, Wetwang. The village boasts two pubs, two craft shops, a post office and shop. Most of St. Nicholas' church is thirteenth century or later, although some older fragments survive, including a Norman font.

Those wishing to press on should turn right along Southfield Road, and right again at the T-junction down Southfield Well Balk, which leads you back onto Green Lane one mile south of Wetwang. Turn left and walk along the lane for 300 yards to a bridleway signpost which is almost hidden by the hedge on the left. Turn right through a gap in the hedge and follow the west side of the hedge southwards to the field corner. Turn right, then left after 50 yards at the dew pond, bringing you onto a chalk track which leads south to Angus Farm. Enter the farmyard by the north-west corner and keep straight ahead, between a hut on the left and a belt of trees to the right. The track bends left and right before continuing southwards to join the Huggate-Tibthorpe road (943554).

Walk westwards up the road, turning left after 400 yards at a bridleway signpost pointing along a track on the west side of the hedge. Ignore the track going left just before the end of the first field, and bear slightly right through a gateway before continuing southwards along the field edge into Deep Dale. Turn right at the fence in the valley bottom, then left through a gate in the fence a few yards before reaching another gate in the hedge ahead. A well-defined path turns left and follows the fence eastwards for a few yards, before climbing the hillside through the wood to a handgate. Go through the gate and follow a wire fence south to a dew pond, where you join a chalk track. Follow the track south for just over a mile to North Dalton. This final stretch is downhill, providing a gentle finish for tired legs, and has fine views to the south-east.

Shortly after passing the cricket pitch, ignore the track going left into the farm and keep straight on through a gate and along Hudson's Lane to Main Street. Turn right to walk back to the starting point and well-deserved refreshment.

Stuart Rennie

31

A WALK AROUND FLAMBOROUGH HEAD

Starting point: *Bempton church, Grid Reference 191721*
Distance: *11 miles (5 or 6 hours)*

Maps: *Landranger 1:50,000 Sheet 101*
                 Pathfinder 1:25,000 Sheet 646

Transport: *By train to Bempton by the Hull-Scarborough line,*
                 buses by East Yorkshire Motor Services
                 from Bridlington.

Refreshment: *There are cafés during the summer and a pub, all*
                 the year round, near Thornwick Bay.

A geological map of England shows the pattern of chalk to include, starting from the south, the South Downs from the white cliffs of Dover through to Beachy Head, then the North Downs and the Chiltern Hills. An extension northwards emerges to form the Lincolnshire Wolds and continues north of the Humber estuary as the Wolds of East Yorkshire which, with their typical grassland dry valleys, give so many splendid walking opportunities. This northern run of chalk terminates eastward in the magnificent white cliffs of Flamborough Head which, in 1979, was defined as Heritage Coast.

At all seasons of the year Flamborough Head is a most exhilarating and interesting area for walking. Many visitors just travel by car and do not venture very far from the popular parking places; they miss so much. A variety of walks is possible because the headland can be likened to part of a wheel with cliffs at the rim and spokes running out from Flamborough village at the hub. Walks can easily be planned to take in more or less of the rim.

Anyone visiting this headland should first take heed of three serious warnings. First, keep safely away from the cliff top edges as the grass surface can be dangerously undercut by chalk and soil erosion to the point of breaking away. Also, a careless slip on mud or wet grass can be impossible to stop. Lives have been lost. Second, at beach level keep well away from the cliff face as there is always the possibility of chalk rocks falling from above. Third, beware of the tides. The height of the tide varies through the year; some are much higher than others and therefore come in faster. Tide times and heights can be ascertain-

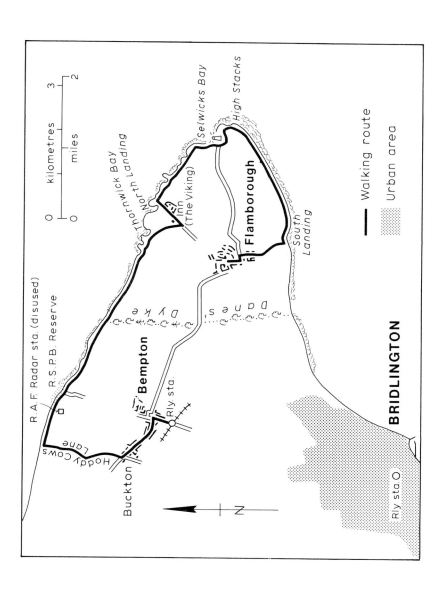

ed in advance, so don't take chances and get cut off by a rising tide at the foot of a cliff. Rescue services are all too often exercised on account of people taking chances in ignorance. However, with sensible behaviour there should be no unfortunate incidents.

A good eleven mile walk may be accomplished in 5 or 6 hours by starting at Bempton and finishing at Flamborough. These villages are $2^1/_2$ miles apart, but by taking the train (Hull-Scarborough line) from Bridlington to Bempton Station and returning by the regular bus service from Flamborough village to Bridlington an hour of extra road walking is avoided. Alternatively, if a party is using two or more cars one can be left at Flamborough village to return drivers to the other car(s) at Bempton.

From Bempton Church walk three-quarters of a mile westwards along the road to Buckton. Turn right into Hoddy Cows Lane (182728) heading northwards past the pond and an area of gorse bushes towards the cliffs, which are up to 400 feet in height. Beyond the two gates of a fenced cattle compound follow the fence on your left hand side. Turn right along the clifftop path (eastwards) for a walk which reveals a continuous panorama of interesting features around the headland. The path is well signposted and provided with stiles and steps where necessary. The features appear in the following sequence.

Above Bempton cliffs is a disused RAF radar station (in use from 1940 until 1967). Next is the only mainland gannet colony in Britain. The RSPB have provided a safety fence for the viewing area which is visited by a great many birdwatchers each year. Most activity can be seen in May, June and July to cover the breeding season. Nesting and the feeding of young can be closely observed using binoculars. Telephoto lenses are much in evidence.

The RSPB reserve has other safety-fenced viewing areas along the path where literally hundreds of seabirds may be observed either in flight, on the water or in their various colonies at different levels of the cliff faces, mainly the kittiwake, puffin and guillemot, also herring gulls, cormorants and shag, plus jackdaws, starlings and pigeons. An RSPB information centre is just one field away from the cliff path. The Protection of Birds Act 1954 saw the end of the centuries old practice of "climming" down the cliffs on ropes to collect eggs.

Following the cliff path again, one can try to identify features having interesting names on the map, eg Crab Rocks, Scale Nab, Cat Nab. It is at the latter point that the route crosses the north end of Danes Dyke. This man-made defensive earthwork, 60 feet wide in parts, was constructed to safeguard the end of the headland (about five square miles). It runs from the northern sea cliffs southwards for two miles to a pre-glacial ravine on Bridlington Bay. It is believed to date from the Iron Age, 2000 or more years ago. Having passed the Dyke look back at it from the defenders' side.

As you proceed along the path, other landmarks come into view and there is always interest seawards. Fishing boats, boats carrying sea anglers, boats tending crab and lobster pots which have their positions marked by flagged floats, cargo ships further out, sailing boats (perhaps from The Royal Yorkshire Yacht Club at Bridlington), maybe a practice exercise between an RNLI lifeboat and a yellow painted RAF air/sea rescue helicopter from Leconfield, near Beverley. Botanists will also be looking at the particular plants and flowers which thrive in these exposed cliff-top conditions.

The next point of note is Thornwick Bay, where there is access down to the beach. Here is about the half-way mark of this walk. A café stands above the bay. It meets seasonal demand and may be open at some weekends in spring or autumn, but is usually closed for the winter. However, bearing away to the right is "The Viking" public house which has welcomed walkers out of season as well as in. There are tables and benches outside where picnic lunches and pints have been known to coincide. The pub is on the road leading to North Landing, one of the principal tourist attractions. Fishing boats, known as cobles, are here winched out of the water to a slope above the beach. The RNLI Lifeboat Station is well worth a visit and is usually open to the public. The record of rescues gives an indication of the perils of the sea on this part of the coast, which has been described as a maritime graveyard. The seabed around the Head and northwards is littered with wrecks. These include coal carriers, U-boats, fishing and other vessels from several centuries.

The cliffs hereabouts have been sculptured by nature to form buttresses, pillars, arches and caves, the latter reputed to have been used by smugglers in days gone by. To cater for visitors, North Landing has a modern building including a cafeteria, gift shop, licensed bars and ice-cream kiosk adjacent to an extensive car park and public toilets. Our route takes us past and around the end of this building following the path close to the cliff near some bungalows.

Then appear some features identifiable from the map as Breil Nook, Cradle Head and Stottle Bank Nook until Selwicks Bay is reached. This is the lighthouse area where there are several interesting things to be seen. A plaque and toposcope commemorate a sea battle which took place off Flamborough Head in 1779 during the American War of Independence. Four American ships commanded by the privateer John Paul Jones were attacking merchantmen sailing under British protection. The two English men-of-war, Serapis and the Countess of Scarborough commanded by Captain Richard Pearson held the Americans to allow the merchantmen to escape but, being outgunned, were forced to surrender after five hours fighting. However, the American flagship, the Bonhomme Richard, sank the following day.

John Paul Jones is revered by Americans as a hero and father of the present US Navy. The toposcope indicates the direction and distance of many places, John O'Groats and Lands End being equidistant at 362 miles! The octagonal chalk tower seen slightly inland on the Flamborough road was a beacon lighthouse built in 1674. The present operational lighthouse, 85 feet high, was built in 1806. Nearby is a café and gift shop, open to meet seasonal and weekend demand. Beyond the lighthouse are public toilets on the track leading to the fog signal station which was built in 1859. The siren emits two blasts every $1\frac{1}{2}$ minutes in foggy weather. This can alarm the unsuspecting visitor as it is extremely powerful.

At a short distance further on is High Stacks where there is now a proper path with steps leading down to the beach. If, and only if, the tide is going out or at its lowest, there is the option of safely walking along the beach for a distance of almost two miles. Allow at least an hour for this. The beach is partly smooth slabs with occasional sand, gravel and rocky stretches. At the foot of the cliff are fallen chalk lumps, many smoothed and rounded by the action of the sea. Beware of slippery seaweed. This 'south coast' of Yorkshire is delightful with winter sun shining on the white chalk cliffs and at other times of the year.

If in any doubt about the tide then keep to the cliff top path which will bring you to South Landing as well as giving splendid views over Bridlington bay as you walk.

At South Landing is a new Heritage Coast Information Centre complete with public toilets. From there it is only a $\frac{3}{4}$ mile walk up the road to Flamborough Village. A turn to the left and then to the right will bring walkers to the village centre. The service buses usually arrive from North Landing and the Lighthouse alternately and stop to pick up near the Royal Dog and Duck public house on their way to

Bridlington. If time allows, read the inscription on the Fisherman's Memorial across the road. It records a 1909 story of bravery and tragedy in strong seas.

With so much to see it may be that time runs out. In that event the walk can be shortened to 9 miles by following the road from the lighthouse direct to Flamborough village.

A booklet is on sale at the Heritage Coast Information Centre, describing circular walks on Flamborough Head. This gives more detail on certain sections of the walk. It can be obtained in advance from the Heritage Coast Project Officer, 4-6 Victoria Road, Bridlington (Tel 0262 678967).

Before you start, do check the tide times, even if you are not venturing along the beach. If you happen to be there at the right time you will see why the fishing boats leave to get back into Bridlington Harbour before the tide runs out. There can be a long wait for those that miss it.

And don't forget to take your binoculars and camera!

Dennis Parker

A RAMBLE IN HULL'S OLD TOWN

Starting point: *Town Docks Museum, Queen Victoria Square, Grid Reference 096287*

Distance: *about two hours*

Map: *a street map of Hull*

Transport: *Buses and trains, less frequent on Sundays*

Refreshment: *various cafés and pubs*

For this walk we leave the countryside and enter the urban environment of Kingston upon Hull (to give the city generally known as Hull its official name) and in doing so we follow a national trend back to rambling about our towns and cities.

During the 19th century some fine descriptive guides were published that suggested walks both in Hull and the surrounding areas. However, in the later years of that century and throughout the twentieth there has been an 'instinctive' desire to be out and about in the countryside while the cities became something of a ramblers' void. Hull was not totally neglected. Thomas Stainforth, one of our founder members, for example, continued to comb the byways and riverfronts. When Walter Wilkinson brought his puppets to the city after much rural tramping he thoroughly enjoyed the experience, which he described in his book *Puppets in Yorkshire* published in 1931.

There are over 40 miles of public footpath in Hull, which includes some 15 miles of riverfront. The Holderness Way (21 miles to Hornsea) starts alongside the River Hull at Stoneferry.

Nor do we only have bricks and mortar to show, for as the town and city expanded over the rural landscape all was not lost. Ridge and furrow will be seen by following the medieval green lane known as Great Field Lane at Marfleet off Hedon Road, and the site of a Saxon settlement (G. H. Hill *Township of Newland* 1909) still with open fields in 1987 — known as Haverflatts or 'Farmers Fields' to the local children — can be seen on either side of County Road North flyover just off Priory Road.

There are fresh water dikes teaming with life, the curlew can be seen and heard, wheatears pass within a short distance of the city centre while the beauty of the smew and excitement of orchids can be experienced from dockland footpaths....putting some of the wildlife deserts created by intensive farming to shame.

Start the walk at the Town Docks Museum in Victoria Square. A few yards away to the east is Queens Gardens, originally Hull's first dock, completed in 1778. The opening of this dock was to the delight of customs officers but much to the annoyance and cost of the merchants who were used to unloading their ships in the Old Harbour onto private wharves. Beyond the museum, the cream brick buildings used to house the dock stables (information from Chris Ketchell). The dock was filled in in the thirties.

From the museum cross the road as if going towards Ferens Art Gallery, but once across head away from the square and pass the open north end of Princes Dock, called Junction Dock when first opened in 1829 because it formed a junction between the Humber and Old (later

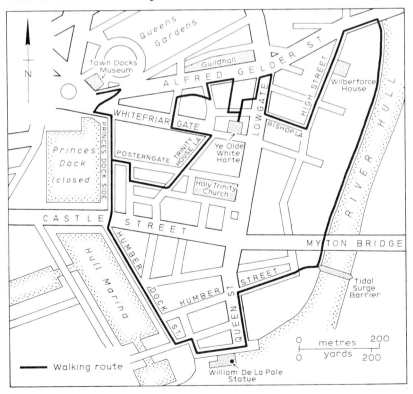

Queens) Docks. The docks took on their more permanent names after a visit by Queen Victoria and Prince Albert in 1850. (Hull also had a Victoria and still has an Albert Dock).

Turn south along Princes Dock Street, passing Commercial Chambers which was built as an alms house, Ferries Hospital (I. and E. Hall *Georgian Hull*, 1978) in 1822 and forms part of the Trinity House Estate. Trinity House School and chapel can be seen through an arch a few yards further on. Soon you will come to Posterngate, which was literally the postern or side gate in the medieval (brick) town wall. Across the way is the Waterfront Hotel, where food and refreshments can be had in the unusual surroundings of this refurbished former warehouse built in 1837. Enter Posterngate and turn first right along Dagger Lane to Prince Street, walk along this restored mid-18th century street through the archway to King Street and the open market facing Holy Trinity Church.

To your right notice the 16th century Grammar School, though it is Holy Trinity that dominates this part of the Old Town. The nature of the underlying soil and peat prevented any massive construction and so today we see a 'lighter' church dating from the 13th century, (information from Mr. William Foot Walker). A walk around Holy Trinity would reveal considerable brickwork, reflecting an important aspect of old Hull, for as the town was too distant from supplies of good building stone and as suitable building clay was available locally, brick buildings predominated. The medieval town hall incorporated 4,700,000 bricks (Kingston upon Hull Museums *Bulletins* 3 and 4 (1971)).

From Prince Street head left into Trinity House Lane and notice the Trinity House building dated 1793. Notice also ahead of you a bend in the street and that if you look backwards you see more bends. The reason is that this is the mid section of the ancient Beverley Street which originally formed a single highway but is now made up of Sewer Lane, Fish Street, King Street, Trinity House Lane and Land of Green Ginger. It has been suggested that Beverley Street pre-dates Hull —Kingston upon Hull dates from 1293 and may have previously existed as Wyke. ('Excavations in Sewer Lane Hull, 1974' in *East Riding Archaeologist* Vol 3, (1977)).

Continue until you reach Whitefriargate, so named because the Trinity House Estate is built on what was a Carmelite or White-Friary, and walk down until Parliament Street is on your right. At this point look across to the Boots building, which was built as the

Holy Trinity Church
Hull

41

Neptune Inn in 1794...can you see Neptune? Notice also the VR post box, said to be the oldest in Hull. Enter Parliament Street, so called because it needed an Act of Parliament to develop it in 1795 and which development removed, among others, Mug House and White Dog entries. Here used to be the Police Station, Stamp Office and Inland Revenue. Next to Wigfalls, but now with a Victorian front, was the first purpose built Subscription Library.

Initially the street looks to be built as a single terrace but closer inspection shows slight variations on each individual plot. Some still retain their original balconies, windows, rain water heads and fall pipes. See also the door casings which are made out of wood and not stone. A little before the end of the street, immediately past number 2 on the right, enter the narrow passage and continue to Duncan's Place. Incidentally, number 2 was built for one Aistroppe Stovin, Attorney, who was instrumental in obtaining the necessary Act of Parliament. Follow Duncan's Place to the street beyond, passing as you do the former Duncan Arms, the last building on your left...now alas dry! You should now find yourself in Manor Street, near to where the manor house used to be. Turn left to the Burlington Tavern, one of the few 18th century buildings left in this part of town and what stories it could tell... Across the way are the Law Courts and Guildhall dating from c1915. Alfred Gelder Street is also relatively modern and prior to its and Guildhall's construction there stood, in my opinion, a superior Town Hall and narrow Broadley Street.

From Manor Street turn right until you come to an archway which leads to The Pathway and pass through into the 'court'. This was originally Cook's Buildings or Square and was developed c1792 by a gaoler, Thomas Cook. Only a single building of that period remains. Opposite that once stood a public house originally named the Hull Gaol, later the Bird in Hand, then (c1840) the Royal William and by the late 1850s the Providence House, but by that time a mere beer house. The buildings facing as you walk through the alley are 18th century (property deeds in my possession). On entering Bowlalley Lane head left for a few yards to the impressive Cogan Chambers and Exchange Alley.

Turn into this alley and follow its course until you emerge onto a busy thoroughfare, Lowgate, but notice in passing the building on the corner and on your left. This was the site of the Exchange and News Rooms, set up in 1794 by one of Hull's most colourful and controversial characters, William Bell, 'Auctioneer and sometime Gent'...He died in 1823. If refreshments are required a diversion can be taken at this point and the route rejoined afterwards. Soon after the corner is turned notice on your right a well worn step leading to an unnamed entry. Take this way back to Bowlalley Lane and look for the sign of the White Hart. Go along this alley to the White Hart Inn, a building of mid 17th century origin (I. and E. Hall, *Georgian Hull*). This may have been the abode of the Governor of Hull and legend has it that on a dreary April day in 1642, in the room known today as the Plotting Chamber, the then Governor, Sir John Hotham, took the momentous decision to refuse King Charles 1 entry to the town. This refusal was the first open act of rebellion against the King at the commencement of the Civil War.

After leaving Exchange Alley turn left and walk to the end of Lowgate, cross the road and head back towards the 14th century church of St. Mary. You will see that the street actually passes through the west tower. This feature was added when the church was 'improved' in the early 1860s by the eminent architect Gilbert Scott. Carry on until Bishop Lane (site of the Bishop's house or palace) is reached and follow this to High Street. At the end of the lane turn left, passing the Transport and Archeology Museum, Maister House and the recently built and refurbished buildings which include a much-needed Bistro.

Behind these buildings used to be many little courts, entries, squares and yards and through one of the surviving arches was Vine Court where the afore-mentioned William Bell lived in the late 18th century. Such 'courts' were common throughout old Hull and were usually infill behind the more prosperous frontages. Pass Wilberforce House and the double Georgian Houses now forming a museum, and the restored warehouses once declared 'beyond repair' but which now house flats, and at the end of the street turn right towards Drypool Bridge but do not cross over. Instead go down the steps onto the riverside walkway. Keep this course to the Tidal Surge Barrier which was built to prevent the Old Town area from flooding during exceptionally high tides. There is so much to see along this stretch, not only the warehouses dating from the 1660s but also the rivercraft.

At the Surge Barrier rejoin the road and follow Humber Street, originally known as the Back and Fore Ropery. Along this street used to be the southern town walls and the Humber flowed to its base. Here also used to be the principal entrance to the town from the riverside and the Half Moon Battery or South End...all gone without trace or care!

Shadows on the River Hull. Photo by courtesy of Roy Dresser.

At the cross roads turn left towards the River Humber and along Queen Street to Corporation Pier. The ferry no longer sails but there is still much to do and see from this area. Keep to the waterside and soon you will come to the Marina (formerly Humber Dock, opened in 1809, and Railway Dock opened in 1846). This area is still not fully developed but it is once again a lively place. All you need to do now is to keep walking with the waterside to your left, across the 'motorway', until you arrive back at Victoria Square.

Roy Dresser

THIXENDALE AND WHARRAM PERCY

Starting point: *Thixendale, Grid Reference 845610*

Distance: *Long Walk - 13½ miles (5½ hours)*
Short Walk - 9½ miles (4 hours)

Maps: *Landranger 1:50,000 Sheets 100 and 101*
Pathfinder 1:25,000 Sheet SE86/96

Parking: *in the village.*

Refreshment: *All in Thixendale. Public House Cross Keys, Tetley's Ales). Cream Teas and bed and breakfast at 'Round the Bend' cottage, YHA Hostel, village shop and Post Office.*

Thixendale is set in the very heart of the East Yorkshire Wolds and was described by the walker and author, A. J. Brown, as 'a land of broad acres' and 'of gentle ridges with immense vistas of undulating arable land, acres and acres of corn and green pastures'. He also described the area as 'Yorkshire at its richest and best' and listed sixteen dales which converge on the village of Thixendale — from Brubberdale to Waterdale and Williedale to Buckdale.

This walk passes through several of these dales, along part of the old Brough to Malton Roman road, along the ancient Aldro Bridleroad and through the deserted village of Wharram Percy. It also follows part of the Wolds Way, a long distance footpath for which the local Ramblers' Association campaigned and fought for many years, against the opposition of several local landowners. The walk also crosses three of the very large Wolds Estates: the Garrowby Estate, the Raisthorpe Estate and the Birdsall Estate. Again the RA in East Yorkshire has spent many, many hours fighting for the rights of way on these estates and much time negotiating with the landowners and their agents. Agreement has been reached with both the Garrowby and Raisthorpe Estates and their paths can now all be walked. Unfortunately with the Birdsall Estate public inquiries have had to be held to prove rights of way, including those to Wharram Percy, and there are still many footpaths resisted by this large estate, in some of the finest walking country in East Yorkshire.

Park (considerately, of course) somewhere in the village and walk to the western end near Manor Farm. About 100 yards past the farm turn left through a gate and follow the path up the bottom of Thixendale. After two gates turn right through a bridlegate and walk up Milham Dale. Towards the top of this dale follow the track right to a field gate. Go through this and turn left along the farm access track.

At the public road turn right and walk along this Roman Road. Here there are excellent views across the Vale of York. A glance at the OS map reveals that this area is rich in ancient burial sites with a long barrow and many tumuli. The barrow measured 80 feet by 2 feet high and was excavated in the 19th century. It had a large timber facade in the eastern end and four early neolithic pots were found in the barrow. At the next junction turn left (signposted Hanging Grimston), walk past the farm and at the sharp bend turn right through a gate. There are now views of the Howardian Hills on your left. After one field cross a stile and at the top of the dale go through a gate, turn left along the road and after 15 yards turn right.

Walk down the field ahead and in the corner go through two bridlegates. Turn right immediately along the bottom of Brownmoor Dale, past a dew pond and to the gate which leads to the road in Birdsall Dale. Turn left and follow the road to Aldro Farm.

At the farm turn right along the ancient bridleroad (signposted Vessey Pasture and Toisland). The track is metalled at first but soon becomes a chalk track. Where the chalk road turns sharply to the left the Wolds Way Long Distance Path is joined. (You can turn right here to follow the waymarked path back to Thixendale if you feel like shortening the walk to about $8\frac{1}{2}$ miles). However, most walkers will want to visit Wharram Percy, so continue ahead along the now grassy track. There will now be a tree belt on your right. Where these trees finish opposite Wharram Percy Farm there is a waymarked bridleway off to your right past the ruins of Wold House Farm. This is the short route back to Thixendale. See later for details of this short route.

For the longer walk visiting Wharram Percy continue ahead along the right-hand edge of the grassy dale with first a hedge and then another tree belt on your right. Soon follow the beautiful Deep Dale around to your left with views of the ruined church and Wharram Percy deserted village site coming into view. Near the village the path goes down the dale side where you cross a stile near the top end of the

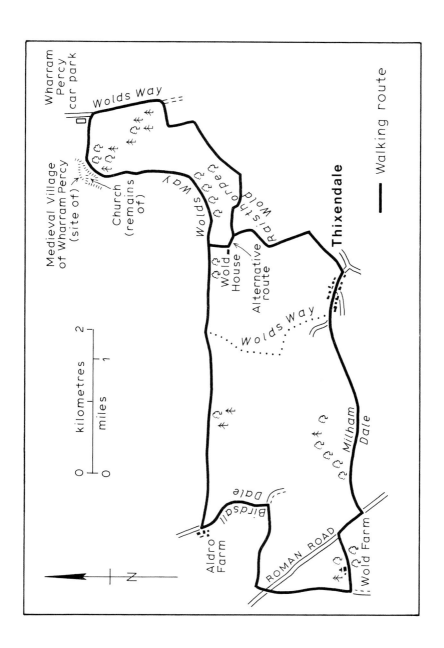

Wharram Percy car park

Wolds Way

Medieval Village of Wharram Percy (site of)

Church (remains of)

Wolds Way

Raisdale Wold

Wold House

Alternative route

Thixendale

Wolds Way

Milham Dale

Birdsdale Dale

Aldro Farm

ROMAN ROAD

Wold Farm

N

kilometres
0   1   2

miles
0   1

—— Walking route

Thixendale village. Photo by courtesy of David Rubinstein.

restored village pond.

The path goes through the churchyard and past the cottage. After a kissing gate to the left of the cottage you follow a chalk track up and then down through the village site to the old disused railway line. Wharram Percy is by far the best of the deserted village sites in the East Riding of Yorkshire and excavations are carried out annually during the month of July. The site is now maintained and administered by the Department of the Environment and they have recently erected many information boards and plaques explaining the remains and history of the village. A medieval woodland is being restored and the medieval pond, as we have seen, has already been reconstructed. The ruined church, used into this century, is sited on the remains of an earlier Anglo-Saxon nave. The village is on the 'Ramblers' Wolds Way' where the RA had to agree to differ with the official, in our view much inferior, route. But virtually all users opt for the Ramblers' version of this Long Distance Path, going through the village and up the Deep Dale footpath, rather than by the official route which follows the metalled road above Bella Farm.

To continue, cross the old railway line using two wooden kissing gates (off to your right is the old Burdale railway tunnel). Follow the path onto a chalk track and up via a gate and stile to Wharram Percy village car park. Here turn right along the metalled road. Where the

Wharram
Percy

metalled road bears right and then sharp left continue up the grassy chalk track on the left-hand side of Wharram Percy Wold Wood (signposted Wolds Way). About 200 yards after the wood turn left off the track.

Follow the field edge (with the hedge to your right) and in the second field turn right through a metal gate. Continue with a hedge to your right and at the end of the field join a grass track. About 300 yards past a wood on your right turn right through a bridleway gate. Walk up the right-hand side of the grassy bank ahead and bear right at the top of the field. Follow the hedge on your left until it finishes where you turn through 90 degrees to walk across the field, taking your bearings from the ruins of Wold House (head just to the left of the ruins). Soon you join a chalk track at the bottom on a grassy slope — the short walk route joins here.

Turn left and walk down the track. Pass one farm track on your right and at the first good hedge turn right. Keep the hedge on your right. At Court Dale go through a bridlegate and turn left along the left-hand side of the dale. At the end of the dale go down and through a bridleway gate. In 50 yards turn right and walk up the edge of a grassy bank. Cross a stile and walk ahead across a grass field to a stile and gate which gives access to the village of Thixendale.

Geoff Eastwood

A WALK ALONG THE MINSTER WAY - STAMFORD BRIDGE TO YORK

Starting point: *Stamford Bridge, Grid Reference 711556 or Kexby Bridge, 705551*

Distance: *Long Walk - 16 miles (about 6 hours)*
Short Walk - 12 miles (4½ hours)

Maps: *Landranger 1:50,000 Sheet 105*
Pathfinder 1:25,000 Sheets SE75,65 and 64

Transport: *by East Yorkshire Motor Services bus from York to Kexby*

Refreshment: *Stamford Bridge, Kexby Bridge, Fulford and York.*

It is now more than ten years since the idea of a long distance path between the Minsters of Beverley and York entered my mind. I suppose it was quite a revolutionary idea, as we had no other Long Distance Paths in our area at the time. The Wolds Way, had of course, been uppermost in our thoughts for many years, but approval by official bodies was long overdue.

Perhaps impatience on my part, impatience with this lack of progress, and with some of the route descriptions which I had suffered whilst trying to follow other paths, was the spur which I required to embark on the fascinating task of exploring the rights of way and pestering the County Councils to bring them into a proper condition for walkers to use. Whatever it was that started me off, the Minster Way has been a part of my life ever since, and has given pleasure to many other walkers (pain to only a few).

The encouragement and help, so freely given by RA members such as Richard Kenchington, erstwhile Footpath Secretary, and originator of the Derwent Way, and Alan Killick, who was later to pioneer the Hull Countryway, proved invaluable. It is a pity that the many people who have enjoyed the route throughout the eighties may not realise how much work was done by the RA in establishing routes such as these. Whether they do or not, the Minster Way has been enjoyed by many and is still there to be walked, almost a decade after the guidebook was first published, and is in much better condition than it was then. It is waymarked and easy to follow. With this in mind, the text below is a description of what is probably the least-known section of the Way, crossing the peaceful countryside between Stamford Bridge and York.

The walk starts at the bridge over the River Derwent at Stamford Bridge (711556), and ends at the south door of York Minster (602523). If you wish to shorten the walk to a mere 12 miles, catch the Beverley bus from York (outside the railway station) to Kexby Bridge (705551) and walk back. I think you will enjoy the experience.

Leaving the bridge at Stamford, walk south along the east bank of the Derwent, at first on a narrow path between a fence and the river, passing under the old railway bridge after a few hundred yards (beware pigeons!). It would take a walker of special talents to get lost here, just follow the river faithfully all the way to Kexby Bridge, enjoying not only the river and its wildlife, but also the healthy exercise provided by climbing the thirty or so stiles which you will encounter.

On reaching the A1079 Beverley to York road, turn right along the footway for a 150 yards, turning right immediately past a café along a gravel track going north. After half a mile, this becomes an unsurfaced path, usually well-defined, going straight ahead to meet a hedge. Go through the gap in the hedge and turn left, on a broad path leading into, and through a wood. Emerge into the sunshine (hopefully!) and follow the surfaced track ahead, until you again meet the York road at Scoreby Lodge.

Exercise care crossing this road to gain the farm track at the other side, which follows south past the farmhouse on your left, White Carr Farm. Do not turn towards the farm but continue straight ahead until, a hundred yards past the farmhouse, the surfaced farmtrack turns right along the bed of the old Selby-York railway. Do not follow the track to the right, but continue straight ahead from the bend into the wood ahead, on an unsurfaced path. This wood, called Rabbit Warren, is a good place for a stop. Squirrels may be seen here, as well as a variety of birds.

The track soon emerges from the wood and follows its eastern edge, south towards Kexby Stray Farm (679494). Turn right just before reaching the farm, following a surfaced track for half a mile to the B1228 road.

Turn right onto the road and follow it north-west for a quarter of a mile. On your left you will see Gypsey Wood Farm. At the end of the

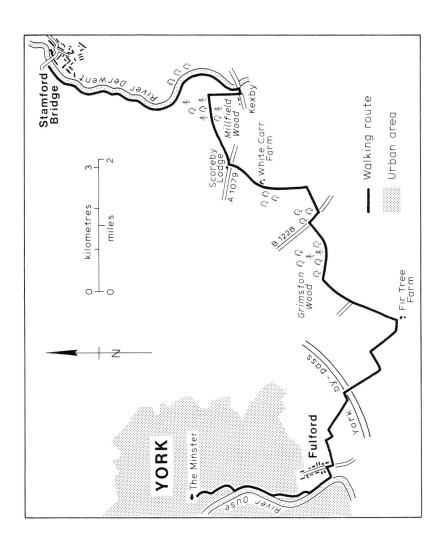

53

long fence in front of the farm, turn left along a track (670494). This swings left after a few yards, but your route is straight ahead, between an archway of trees, on an unsurfaced track. On emerging from the trees, turn right at Gypsey Corner (664489) and turn right (west-north-west) along the grassy path between the stream on your left and the southern edge of Grimston Wood on your right. The stream turns left (south-west) at the southwest corner of the wood, and you should follow its right-hand bank, first on a rough grass track then inside the boundaries of three fields, before continuing ahead on a 150 yards of grass track to reach the road known as Langwith Stray (851485).

Take this straight road south-south-west for three quarters of a mile. Where it bends left towards Fir Tree House, walk straight ahead for about fifty yards. Walk west, straight across the field (often ploughed) to a rather dilapidated footbridge crossing Tillmire Drain. Turn right north-west with a fence and the drain on your right. On your left is Tillmire Common. Several applications to plough and fence this land have so far been resisted.

Three hundred yards from the bridge, the drain slants right, but you should stay alongside the fence on your right for a further third of a mile to enter the boundary of Fulford Golf Course through a six-foot-wide gate. Go through the gate, close it, and turn left along a clear sandy track which leads you to the southwestern corner of the course, where turn right (north west) between the fairways on your right and a ditch on the left, keeping an eye open for low-flying golf balls. If the weather is clear, York Minster can be seen in the distance, directly ahead and framed by trees, so you must be walking in the right direction!

You will soon become aware of the sound of traffic on the dual carriageway of the York bypass ahead. Just before reaching the road, turn right along the boundary fence to gain the bridge crossing the busy road. After crossing this bridge follow the track round to the right, past a pylon and back to the boundary fence of the road. By walking to the left for a few yards along the fence, you will reach a turn right (south west) along the side of the road for a nerve-wracking 250 yards, to where there is a small concrete bridge and a stile on your right (just before the layby), taking you northwest away from danger and into the edge of a plantation (627483).

At the end of the trees, cross the ditch on your right and resume your north-westerly direction, keeping the ditch on your left. About a half mile after the plantation, the track you are following turns left (west-south-west). This track, shown on old maps as Germany Lane, meets another at a T-junction. Turn right (north-west) here, taking one more turn to the left before following the lane west to the A19 road in Fulford, next to Fulford Mews (611488).

Turn right alongside the roadside footway for 60 yards or so. On reaching Glen Close, just before the Bay Horse, cross the main road and walk between two detached houses, numbered 114 and 120, to reach a footpath alongside gardens. The path between these two houses looks private, but isn't, yet all attempts to have it signposted by North Yorkshire Council have so far been unsuccessful. Why not drop them a line and encourage them?

Follow the stream to your left, down to the River Ouse, turn right (north west) along the river bank and follow the grassy path towards York. Half a mile along the river, a large modern boathouse is reached. The right of way goes to the left of this, then follows a wall to the right, but as this path is usually obstructed with rubbish, you may prefer to take the more obvious path to the right, just before the boathouse, taking the lane to the left, in front of the Water Authority's pollution control depot.

Go north, along Love Lane past the former St. Oswald's church, now converted to a private residence. The path returns you to the River at New Walk (603503).

Half a mile along the river, you come to the confluence of the Rivers Ouse and Foss. There is a footbridge known as Blue Bridge here, over the Foss. Turn right after crossing it, past St. George's Field car park on your right and under Skeldergate Bridge. Journey's End, (York Minster) can be seen as can Clifford's Tower on a green mound. You will soon be on King's Staith and will see Ouse Bridge ahead. Turn right along King Street before reaching the bridge, and walk up the slope to Nessgate, which you should cross into Coppergate, the home of the famous Viking centre. Cross Piccadilly, into Pavement and enter the Shambles on your left. At the end of this picturesque thoroughfare, turn into King's Square, then along Low Petergate to reach York Minster via Minster Gates, the short street on your right.

I hope that this section of the Minster Way has provided you with a pleasant day's walking, and that you have been encouraged to complete the whole route as described in my book *The Minster Way* (available from the local RA). The route provides a good introduction to the East Yorkshire countryside and has opened the eyes of many walkers over the years, especially those who have travelled from distant parts of the country to complete it. A badge is available to anyone who has walked the whole route, whether in one burst of energy or in half-mile bits. All walking is a pleasure - enjoy it in whatever way suits you best!

Ray Wallis

A WALK IN WELTON DALE

Starting point: *Welton, Grid Reference 959274*

Distance: *4 miles (about 2 hours)*

Maps: *Landranger 1:50,000 Sheet 106*

Transport: *by East Yorkshire Motor Services bus from Hull*

Refreshment: *Welton.*

This short walk is suitable for children as there are places to run around, plenty of changing interest, a small section of woodland to walk through and both a stream, and a pond. There are some stiles though, so if a dog accompanies you it needs to be able to negotiate these.

Welton itself is now a dormitory village of the city of Hull, and is approached by taking the turning marked 'Welton' from the A63. There are frequent buses from Hull; alight at the Green Dragon pub or by the church 50 yards away.

To start the walk go to the church of St. Helen, near the village centre; there is a pleasant meandering stream nearby, maybe some mallards too. The church has a 13th century chancel, whilst outside is the refurbished headstone marking where Jeremiah Simpson was buried in the 18th century. Read it carefully. He had an interesting claim to local fame for he 'hath eight times married been'. There is also a stone pump on the village green.

Head north-west away from the Green Dragon and the church, past Kidd Lane and into Dale Road. The telephone kiosk on the verge will help with direction finding. This kiosk belongs to Kingston upon Hull Corporation Telephones - the only independent telephone company in the country. The road is marked as a dead end, but that only applies to motorists and means the walker can have a safe, more pleasant route away from the internal combustion engine. There is a Welton Hall sign up a drive near the phone box whilst across the road can be seen a Georgian residence with some reconstructed gas lamps. About 100 yards up from the phone box look for the 'Old Stables House' on your right. Through the gate can be seen an ancient cattle well which you are entitled to use although at your own risk. Keep

57

Ramblers in Welton Dale. Photo by courtesy of Ray Wallis.

looking to the right where a tall building can be seen. This is marked as 'mill' on the Ordnance Survey map - it was probably a water mill.

Keep up the slight incline through the houses to a wooden gate where there are lots of waymarks and a carved Wolds Way finger post, as part of this route follows the Long Distance Path. (You may have already noted a sign for the Wolds Way on the triangle of grass opposite the phone box). There is another sign on the right side of the road indicating that this is a public right of way. The watery area behind the trees on the right (I hesitate to call it a pond) can look attractive with spring flowers and sometimes there are ducks as well. This 'pond' is on forestry land and at its furthest extremity is used as a trout farm although this cannot be seen from the road.

Continue on this tarmacked road to Dale Cottage which is quite an isolated homestead. On the left, just before the cottage which is on the right, if you peep through the trees, you may be able to see a weir; it is certainly possible to hear it. There is also an Artesian well — marked as 'Springs' on the map. A white-painted gate just beyond the cottage leads to Welton Dale. A stile on the left bears a waymark with an extra sticker for the Humber Bridge Link Walk. On the gatepost is an

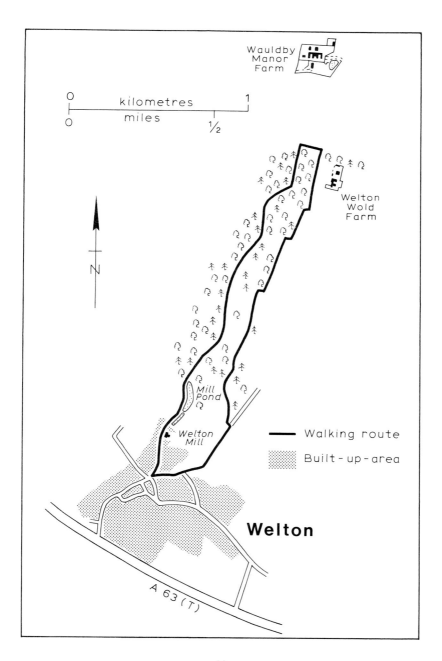

Wauldby
Manor
Farm

O‾‾‾‾‾‾‾kilometres‾‾‾‾‾‾‾1
O‾‾‾‾‾‾‾‾miles‾‾‾‾‾‾‾½

N

Welton
Wold
Farm

Mill
Pond

Welton
Mill

——— Walking route

Built-up-area

Welton

A 63 (T)

intentionally horrific picture of a lamb, savaged by a dog. This ties in with the fact that one is advised to keep dogs on a lead on a public right of way. The contrast provided by the information that there are loose alsatians at the Cottage teases the mind a little, and in the end, one makes one's own decision. I have never seen sheep in Welton Dale, but dogs chasing them would be an offence.

Welton Dale is a favoured spot, for access to which the local RA fought very hard over a period of 10 years or more. One member was even prepared to spend a Christmas in jail for the cause of the public being able to walk there. The land on the left is forestry land and has Douglas fir trees, with an edging of deciduous trees. Elder, ash, sycamore and beech are all represented behind the fence. The right side is open land with gorse bushes, and sometimes it is possible to see rabbits playing there. It is nearly 1200 yards to the next gate - past a stand of conifer trees on the right. Some saplings have been planted so some care is being taken for the preservation of the beauty of the landscape in the Dale.

Beyond this gate, which is permanently open and has a stile, the wood is on both sides of the pathway and presents quite a different aspect. About 250 yards further on is a wooden footpath sign and the netting of a pheasant farm even further to the left. The footpath is clearly marked to the right and drops down into the enclosing woodland. This path can be slippery and muddy, especially after rain, so take care. There are confirmatory waymarks in a few yards, this time with B20 written on. (I did warn you about Long Distance routes - this one is the Beverley 20, much used by local school and youth groups as a challenge walk). Proceed through the wood about 300 yards to a stile at the top of the slope. Cross the concrete farm road and go over the stile immediately opposite. Turn right — there is a Wolds Way sign for confirmation — and take the field-edge path which runs parallel to the farm road.

At the next Wolds Way sign, in about 200 yards, make a strike for independence and carry straight on, leaving the Wolds Way walkers to turn left through a narrow tree belt. In about 30 yards, there is another stile, on the right, so go over that one. It has plenty of waymarks and stickers (B20 mark too) and straight over the concrete road into another wooded area. This is smaller and sparser and leads quickly to a field edge path with Welton Wold Farm (to where the farm road was going) on the left side across the field.

The field-edge path with a wood on the right side goes about 400

60

yards before a right bend and by then the tall chimney of Capper Pass works can be seen clearly over the crop. Follow the bend and head on again, in the same general direction for about another 500 yards. If you check, the path may yield small flints as these were often deposited at the same time as the chalk of which these Yorkshire Wolds are comprised. The walk continues along a fenced-off avenue, which is more than halfway through the walk. There may be clear views over Welton Dale (up which you have just walked), and in the middle distance, the British Aerospace factory at Brough. In the far distance, the Lincolnshire Wolds can be seen across the Humber. Soon saplings will be obvious on the immediate right; they are in pink boxes for protection - this is not a strange East Yorkshire variety of tree! Continue along this avenue until the path turns left; a large hedge bars the way forward and a B20 sign will also be seen. The next part is about 250 yards long with a high fence on the left. This protects you from the disused quarry. Over yet another stile (you should be getting quite good at negotiating these) which has waymarks upon it, and turn right. There is no real alternative — the quarry gates are on the left.

The part-tarmacked road is a relic of the quarry when it was in operation. In about 400 yards one reaches a real junction. A wooden Wolds Way sign is set well back on the right hand side and indicates that route turns left. Today, we are not so adventurous, preferring to leave a section of that route until better equipped, and continue down the gentle incline on the old road. It is not used by traffic now, so should be safe. At the junction previously mentioned, there was a waymark leading off into the wood between the Wolds Way route and our own. Again, this is part of the B20, and left for another day. If the tide is suitable, you may be able to see some of the notorious shifting sandbanks of the Humber estuary. These can cause shipping an enormous amount of trouble and have led to the Humber Pilot Service with its special examinations. Welton church can also be seen. The lane soon becomes wooded on both sides again; Lime and beech trees can be seen, sloe berries found in their season as can wild roses in their time.

After a further 500 yards a 30 mph sign can be seen, together with some houses. This brings the realisation that the time of isolation is over and probably the quiet that may have gone with it. (If you were accompanied by children, quiet is very unlikely). Continue on the road (or more properly, the tarmacked pavement) and eventually you should see the telephone kiosk near to where this jaunt began. Soon you are back at St. Helen's church, and if refreshment is on your mind the Green Dragon pub is just a little further into the village, opposite the church.

It has associations with John Palmer, alias Dick Turpin, who was arrested here in 1739. He was taken to York and the Assizes and later executed. However, tales vary, and the plaque telling of the events of that year is no longer part of the decor at the pub. The actual reason for his arrest was cattle and sheep rustling — not the 'money or your life' style usually associated with this much-romanticised robber. The pub serves food as well as drink and may provide a pleasant finish to your walk. There is also a village shop near the church.

Sheila M. Smith

A CIRCULAR WALK VIA LEAVENING, BURYTHORPE AND BIRDSALL

Starting point: *Leavening, Grid Reference 781631*

Distance: *10 miles (about 4½ hours)*
                  or two 5 miles (2½ hour) walks

Maps: *Landranger 1:50,000 Sheet 100*
                  Pathfinder 1:25,000 Sheets SE66/76 and SE86/96

Parking: *In the village or to the west of Leavening on the*
                  York road, just after the start of the walk

Refreshment: *Leavening and Burythorpe both have good pubs.*

From the village of Leavening take the York road and look out on your right for a stone plinth carrying the village name. Go through the red metal gate on your right beyond the plinth and make your way uphill close by the hedge. As the view ahead opens up you may pick out landmarks including the Sutton Bank White Horse and several Wolds villages.

Dropping down towards a farm (High Penhowe) look out in the hedge ahead for a stile, cross and turn left then right round the buildings, right again and shortly into the field on your left. Turn right into the corner of the field then left downhill with the hedge on your right. Pass through the gates, pass another farm (Low Penhowe) and down the access road to a lane.

Turn right along the lane then left when you reach the road. In 25 yards find a handgate in the hedge on your right and follow the field side uphill until a grass bank rises in front of you, turn left then right to pass close by Burythorpe Church. This small building perched on the hill is a local landmark and commands a wide view of pleasing, well-kept farmland. A good path goes downhill to the village of Burythorpe.

The ten mile walk continues straight ahead down a lane for approximately a quarter of a mile then turns left along the access track to Hermitage Farm. On approaching the buildings go left in the field and through a gateway into a yard, pass the buildings on your right and emerge through another gateway on to an earth track across a field. When the track stops at a gateway go right round the edge of the next field, left at the corner and at the next corner go between trees to find a bridlegate and stile. A faint track goes straight ahead over the grassland, bear to the left of the wood and you will reach a gate. The track becomes clearer and you will soon pass some imposing stone farm buildings, a reminder of the days when quality was important.

On reaching the road go straight ahead then turn right beneath the comparatively modern church. You are now entering the straggling village of Birdsall. More good stone buildings, pretty cottages and much greenery, trees and open space are features of this estate. The 'big house' is glimpsed and nearby the ruins of the ancient church.

The road takes you round to the right on to a 'T' junction. Follow the road signposted Burythorpe until, at a right-hand bend, a lane leaves to the left. This lane will lead you into a farmyard. Bear left and uphill to pick up a track going half-left over rough grazing, rising gently all the way. When you reach a gate with a green public bridleway sign on the left, go through and turn left to reach a road. Turn right and follow the road downhill into the village of Leavening.

TWO SHORTER WALKS

Leavening - Burythorpe

Use the instructions for the beginning of the ten mile walk from Leavening until you reach the village of Burythorpe. Instead of going straight ahead down the lane turn right along the village street until you reach a sharp right-hand bend. On the left a lane goes downhill past a farm. Take this and follow the track through gates and uphill until you emerge at the top of Leavening Brow, then turn right down the road to the village.

Burythorpe - Birdsall

Pick up the ten-mile walk instructions from the village of Bury-thorpe and follow them to the gate with the bridleway sign on the left. This is near the top of Leavening Brow and you may wish to stop here

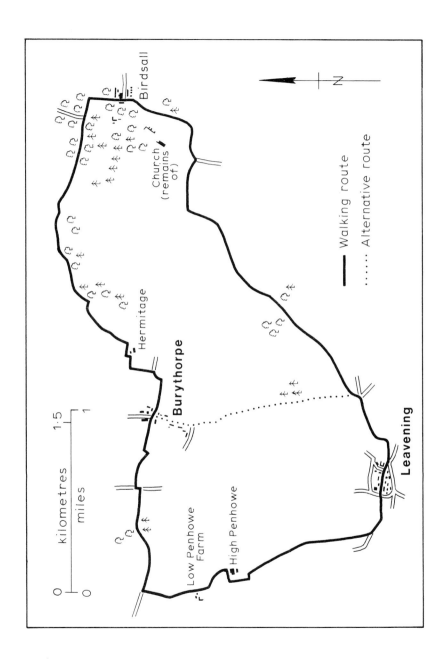

Birdsall

Church (remains of)

Hermitage

Burythorpe

Leavening

Low Penhowe Farm

High Penhowe

Walking route
Alternative route

N

kilometres
1·5
0
miles
1
0

65

a while to admire the view. From the gate turn right downhill on an ancient track, through gates and fields until you reach the village of Burythorpe.

Betty Hood

A CHOICE OF WALKS AROUND SCAMPSTON, WINTRINGHAM, THORPE BASSETT AND RILLINGTON

Starting point: *Scampston, Grid Reference 875753*

Distance: *12 miles (about 5 hours)*
8 miles (3½ hours)
4 miles (2 hours)

Maps: *Landranger 1:50,000 Sheets 100 and 101*
Pathfinder 1:25,000 Sheet SE87/97

Parking   *There is space for parking on the old road at the*
and Transport: *starting point, and the Scarborough-Malton*
West Yorkshire Road Car Co. bus stops nearby.

Refreshment: *Rillington has pubs and a café.*

Walk east along the old road to swing right and join the A64, turn left and in one hundred yards cross the road and follow a stony track uphill. As you near the top look out on your right for a Wolds Way signpost and a narrow path along an earthwork. The view behind you of the Vale of Pickering and the North York Moors is a good excuse to stop and catch your breath before going along the earthwork to a gate. Go through and follow the waymarks carefully as you go downhill. The path turns at several points then goes down the side of a field to emerge at Wintringham Church. At this point the twelve mile walk diverges from the others — see later for details of this route.

The four mile walk here goes left then right round the church and along the village street, a nice mixture of old and new cottages. Beyond the houses a quiet country road takes you straight back to the A64 within sight of your starting point.

The eight mile walk also goes along the village street but near the last houses on the left look out for a lane with a Wolds Way sign. Go over a bridge and follow a well-used path across fields to a lane. Turn left and in a mile, where the main lane swings right into a farm, go forward downhill to a gate and along a grassy track. When the path begins to rise go right round a hedge. Shortly you will see a gate on your right and a track across a field, which you follow. There is a gate near the buildings, go through and turn left to follow the farm access track past a well-kept garden and downhill into Thorpe Bassett.

At the north end of the village street is a sharp left-hand bend, go forward past an access drive and farm buildings along an ancient lane which leads through gates to Rillington. At the traffic lights turn right and soon as possible cross the main road. In 350 yards turn left into Sands Lane and at the road junction bear left to reach the quiet village of Scampston, another group of pretty cottages. Go right then left with the road. On your right find a gateway to the grounds of Scampston Hall and, although this is only a back way through the yard, you will find evidence of the detailed care taken by Capability Brown and his contemporaries who laid out this estate some 200 years ago. Follow the track right then left, cross a bridge then over fields by an avenue of large trees. When you reach the plantation gate go left through bushes to find a stile then right down the side of the field. You will emerge on the A64 a short way from your starting point.

The twelve mile walk leaves Wintringham Church along the road to the east. Follow this for three-quarters of a mile until you find a bridleway going right, uphill. Follow the waymarks carefully beside woodland and along field sides; most of the way is on tracks and elsewhere headlands are wide enough to walk. After passing Ray-slack Farm turn right along the road which is not very busy and with widening views the two miles pass quickly. At Settrington Beacon find a gate and stile on your right onto a forest track and look in the trees to your left for a surprising item! You are once more on the Wolds Way for a short distance. Go right then left to a gate which offers one of many superb views in this area. The grassy track goes downhill to your left to reach a high hedge and trees.

Go left alongside the hedge, through a bridlegate and follow a faint track half left, uphill over rough grazing. On arriving at a new plantation go through two gates then sharp right through a small handgate. The dew-pond on your left has survived from the days of horses, geese and ducks which at one time would populate this old farm yard. The house has gone and only some barns in the traditional chalk and brick style remain to mark Many Thorns Farm.

Go downhill through a gate, bear left off the track dropping steeply at first then as the ground levels make for the right-hand corner of the field. On the rough grazing there are many tracks but sheep and cattle tend not to be interested in keeping to rights of way. Go over the stile and look out on your right for another stile, cross and go forward along the strip between crop and ditch, skirt round the left of a

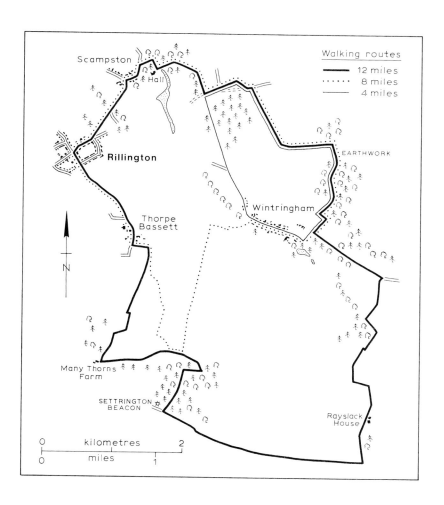

Scampston

Hall

Rillington

Thorpe
Bassett

Wintringham

EARTHWORK

Many Thorns
Farm

SETTRINGTON
BEACON

Rayslack
House

N

Walking routes

━━━ 12 miles

········ 8 miles

─── 4 miles

| O | kilometres | 2 |
| O | miles | 1 |

building and walk north with the hedge on your right. The path goes over several fields, keeping close to the hedge or the stream until you find a stile on your right which brings you to a narrow bridge and out onto a lane. Turn left, follow the lane and you will arrive in Thorpe Bassett. Follow the instructions for the eight-mile walk, given above, from here back to your starting point.

Betty Hood

A CIRCULAR WALK: BRANDSBY - COXWOLD
HUSTHWAITE - BRANDSBY

Starting point: *Cherry Hill, near Brandsby Grid Reference*
                   584726

Distance: *17 miles (about 7 hours)*
                   But can be shortened by using alternative routes

Maps: *Landranger 1:50,000 Sheet 100*
                   Pathfinder 1:25,000 Sheet SE47/57

Transport: *York - Easingwold - Brandsby by Reliance Motor*
                   Services bus
                   York - Easingwold by Reynard Pullman Coaches
                   bus
Refreshment: *Coxwold*

In an area of gentle wooded hills north-east of Easingwold and the Vale of York, this walk, on generally little-used paths, links the picturesque villages of Brandsby, Coxwold and Husthwaite. It passes Byland Abbey in its beautiful setting below the Hambleton Hills and presents a number of dramatic views of the White Horse above Kilburn.

The best place to start is a small road junction (584726) at Cherry Hill, nearly half-a-mile from Brandsby on the road to Crayke, where there is a small grass area suitable for parking. The bus from York to Brandsby will stop here on request. There is a connecting footpath from Brandsby for anyone wishing to start from there.

From the Cherry Hill road junction walk up the minor road then turn right along the farm road to Peel Park Farm. Turn left through double gates before the house, then right. At the end of a concrete roadway turn right again then left over a ditch and immediately left again to a gate with a waymark. Go on along the bottom of a field with a ditch on the left to a gate then bear right diagonally uphill to a stile below the steeper slope. Continue towards the north with a fence then a wood on the right. Approaching a small stream turn right over a stile into the wood. Follow a faint path through the wood with the stream to the left until the stream can be crossed by a grassed bridge near the edge of the wood where there is a stile.

Climb the steep slope beyond to a concrete cistern with a yellow arrow. The arrow indicates a way past a small sewage plant to Yearsley by way of a short concrete road. But this is not the right-of-way which is more to the right towards the highest point, converging on a line of trees. After a wire fence on the left, turn left by climbing the wooden fence (a stile is promised). After a few yards and a gate join a short concrete road with farm buildings on the right into Yearsley village.

In Yearsley turn right then left at the cross roads (a good bus shelter here for wet weather) on the road to Ampleforth. After 500 yards, just before a road junction, turn off right, taking the middle of three tracks. This track crosses cleared woodland, then descends through tall fir trees to join a main track past Yearsley Wood Farm. Another track converges from the left but continue in the same direction downhill through woodland (called The Wilderness). Where the track curves sharply right turn off left on another track then immediately right down a short path with overhanging branches to cross the dam of the top Fish Pond. At the far side turn left on the broad forest track. Another fish pond can be seen through the trees on the left, then the much larger Lower Fish Pond.

Look for a path which leads to the dam at the end of the pond. Walk along the dam then past a boat house to turn left on a metalled road to Redcar House. A few yards before the farm fork off right to a gateway. Now follow a pleasant green track with a fence on the left to the Yearsley/Ampleforth road at 577764. Straight across, continue westerly on a minor road called Colley Broach Road to a junction with the access road to Low Lions Farm. This is the point of divergence for alternative walk 1 described later.

For the full walk continue on the gated road - Byland Abbey can be seen ahead. After crossing the site of an old railway turn right on the access road to Old Pilfit farm. (Alternative walk 2, described later, leaves the main route at the junction). Through the farm a track continues north between fences, waymarked, to the end of Thorpe Spring Wood where a rutted track turns left uphill with a hedge on the right. At the end of the hedge turn left over a cultivated field to a stile about 20 yards to the left of a wood. Over a small beck continue northwest with the wood to the right into a shallow valley.

Go through three gates, a hedge on the left, then emerge into a large pasture with Wass Grange farm to the right. Turn right towards the farm but then curve left with the buildings then trees to the right. After

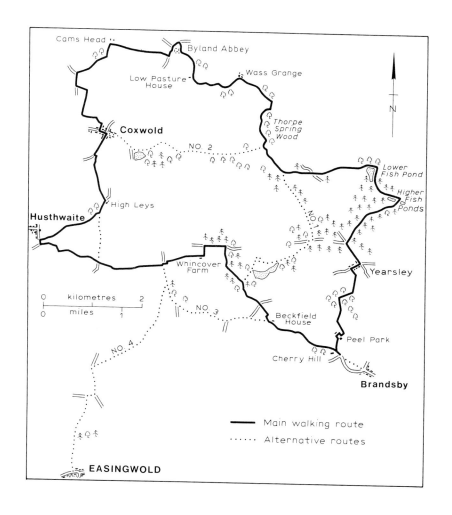

the end of the hedge on the right continue southwest on a faint track on grass with a small hill to the right. About 100 yards from Craykeland Wood turn right with a hedge on the left. Pass through a gate then look for a partly concealed stile in the hedge on the left. The right-of-way is now westerly across a ploughed field to a stile at 556782. Now go uphill with a fence on the right, and good views, past a ruined building above Low Pasture House. Turn right down to a gate in a fence just to the left of a small wood. With the wood to the right continue to a gateway and a track. Follow the track but after a short distance bear slightly right through a gap in the hedge.

Now head for Byland Abbey which can be seen ahead. This is the beautiful monastic ruin of a Cistercian abbey built in the late twelfth and early thirteenth centuries. The church and cloister are larger than those of either Fountains or Rievaulx. There are the remains of a rose window 27 feet in diameter - as large as that of York Minster. Pass to the right of the Abbey and continue in the same direction for a few yards to the road, then turn left.

Take the road for Coxwold, turning off right after 300 yards on a waymarked path to Cams Head where turn left with a hedge on the left down to a wood. Bear right on a vague path along the bottom of the wood. Look for a slab footbridge over a beck and out of the wood. Continue with a hedge on the left to the Oldstead/Coxwold road a little to the south of Fox Folly farm. (There is a right-of-way east of and parallel with the road but a stile and footbridge are required). Turn left (south) on the road for 300 yards then off left along the edge of a cultivated field. Turn right, after another 300 yards, uphill with vestiges of a hedge on the left to a big tree. Go forward with a hedge on the right on a good track with newly planted trees, through a gate then with a line of shrubby trees on the left. Turn left on a faint grassy track eventually with a line of big trees on the right and Coxwold church beyond them.

Go through three kissing gates then turn right up a short lane to emerge in Coxwold main street with the Faulconberg Arms on the right and the village shop opposite. Coxwold is a picturesque village of wide grass verges and interesting buildings including the fifteenth century church with an octagonal tower. Shandy Hall near the church was the home of the 18th century writer Laurence Sterne. Colville Hall and the Old Hall, a former grammar school of 1603, are also fine buildings and Newburgh Priory is only half a mile away.

After refreshment in Coxwold walk down the hill to the crossroads and turn right on the Husthwaite road. About 500 yards along this road a gate on the left gives access to a bridge over a stream. Cross to another gate then turn right keeping the stream on the right until it can be crossed by a footbridge. Over the bridge turn left, uphill, with a hedge on the left. After the hedge slants left bear right a little, uphill. Look for a gap in the hedge ahead. Over a stile in the gap then walk up rough pasture to a gate to the left of a group of trees. Turn right on the road past High Leys farm.

At High Leys the walk can be shortened by continuing up the road and taking the second road on the left to Oulston. Otherwise, after 200 yards of unfenced road, bear right across to trees then left with the trees and a steep slope on the right. The route is now clear - along the top of Beacon Banks with good views of the White Horse and the Hambleton Hills. The path descends past Lists House to a road above the village of Husthwaite. Our route is left on the road but turn off right on a path after a few yards if there is time to visit Husthwaite, an attractive village with a mainly Norman church and some fine houses, including a timber-framed house with a brickwork ground floor.

Turning left on the road at Lists House, turn left again at the road junction a short distance further on. Along a quiet road with high hedges turn right through a gate immediately before the first house on the right — 'The Lodge'. Turn left through a gate with a garden on the left to another gate. Continue the same direction in a field to a gate then bear slightly right to the bottom right-hand corner of the next field. Cross a small stream (no bridge) to a gate at the bottom end of a short lane which may be overgrown. After about 100 yards this lane opens on to a wider lane in which turn left. Go straight across at a cross-roads to a farm road, passing Yeoman House to Oulston.

From Oulston alternatives 3 and 4 described next can be taken, but if you are continuing with the main route turn left on the road for Coxwold then off right after a few yards (just past the entrance to Oulston Hall) on a wide drive. Past a house turn left with farm buildings on the left then right down to a gateway. Continue in the same direction in a field where the path is usually ploughed up. At the top of a slope, Whincover Farm can be seen ahead — aim for it, passing to the left of the buildings. Now follow a farm road which turns left up to a road on which turn right. After 500 yards turn right on a forest track (Brierham Lane). Descend pleasantly through fine trees to a gate then a grassy track with a fence on the right. At the point where there is another wood ahead and a gate on the right with a waymark, the route is to the right, but, if time permits, a diversion of 400 yards to the left here to see Oulston Reservoir, a local beauty spot, would be well worth the effort.

At the bottom of Brierham Lane turn right through the gate and walk downhill to cross the infant River Foss (no bridge) up the slope beyond to a gate to the right of Burton House farm buildings. Join the farm access road next to an electricity pole. With the house to the left walk down the road but slant away right when it bears left, down to a stile. Cross the road to another stile then go across a cultivated field towards farm buildings. Over a small stream curve right with a hedge on the left, looking for a stile in the hedge. In the next field cross to a farm track just to the right of a barn. A few yards forward to a gate, then turn left in the lane past Beckfield House. This lane wanders a little but leads pleasantly, with good views, back to Cherry Hill, our starting point.

Alternative routes.

1. Low Lions and Pond Head - 9 miles.

From the Colley Broach Road on the main route turn off south up the road to Low Lions farm. Through a plantation go forward, the farmhouse to the right, to a gate then bear left to another gate near an electricity pole. Continue in the same direction to converge on a wood. The way is now uphill with the wood to the left. At the top of the wood turn right with a wall on the left to a gate. With fir trees on the right walk up to another gate then on a farm track with High Lions farm on the right to pass through the farmyard by way of two gates. The right-of-way is now down the middle of a field, usually with an arable crop, to a gate at the bottom and a road.

Go right on the Oulston road for 150 yards then off left on a forest track which turns right at the far side of the wood. About 400 yards further on look for an opening in the wood on the right which leads to a bridge over the River Foss near its source. Through a gate, turn left with Pond Head Wood on the left. To get to Pond Head farm which can be seen ahead there is a track on grass curving slightly left then right to a gate. Turn right then left and left again with the farm buildings on the left to a stile.

With a hedge on the right and Oulston Reservoir to the left walk downhill to another stile. Now follow a track, which can be wet, through woodland. This track curves left to the reservoir dam and an attractive view. However, this is not a right-of-way. Instead go back a few yards to find a fainter track leading away from the reservoir to a gate at the edge of the wood. Continue in the same direction with the wood now on the left to the south end of Brierham Lane to rejoin the main route back to Cherry Hill.

2. Via Newburgh to Coxwold - 14 miles

From the Low Lions junction continue on the Colley Broach Road for 2½ miles to Newburgh where turn right for Coxwold and the main route.

3. Oulston to Beckfield House via Adam's Field Lane.

This is only slightly shorter than the main route but easier and quicker if the weather deteriorates. Turn right at the road junction in Oulston then left along Adam's Field Lane after about half a mile. Go straight ahead where the access road to Adam's Hall Farm turns left. A twisting overgrown lane leads eventually to a road. Turn left along the road for 500 yards or so then right on a farm road to Beckfield House Farm and the main route.

4. Oulston to Easingwold. - 18 miles

By following the 'Foss Walk' from Oulston to Easingwold the route can be changed to a linear walk of 18 miles. Route cards can be purchased from the Secretary, River Foss Amenity Society. Telephone York 798475.

Colin Coombes

A SPURN HEAD EXPLORATION

Starting point: *Bluebell shop, Kilnsea, Grid Reference 416157*

Distance: *6 miles (about 3 hours)*

Map: *Pathfinder 1:25,000 TA40/41*

Transport: *Connor and Graham buses from Hull to Kilnsea, (Bluebell) infrequently, more often to Easington 3 miles north. Parking, for which a charge is made is available on Spurn.*

Refreshment: *Bluebell shop and a pub in Kilnsea*

This is not a guided ramble like the others in this collection, all of which follow specific routes made up of legal rights of way. Although there is a right of way on Spurn, running along the western edge, there is little consistent visible evidence of it on the ground. Luckily, however, Spurn is one of the few places in this intensively farmed part of the world where you are free to wander about and savour the strangeness of the place. And that is an opportunity you shouldn't miss. There is, therefore, no line of walk marked on the accompanying map and I shall merely suggest a way of walking down the headland mentioning some of the points of interest. The return route I leave to you, and I defy anyone to get lost on a peninsula as narrow as this one.

Having said that, the headland is a nature reserve, run by the Yorkshire Naturalists Union and owned by the Yorkshire Wildlife Trust. Its particular interest in wildlife terms is that it is a key resting place for migrating birds, including some of the rarities which twitchers - fanatical bird watchers - travel miles to see. Because of this you should be particularly aware of the need not to disturb the birds or the vegetation which provides them with food and cover. Stick to established tracks through the dunes and to the beaches. The easy way of getting around is often to use the road, but I cannot advise that you do so any more than is strictly necessary as it is used by motor vehicles. The road is very narrow and the 20 mph speed limit is ignored as comprehensively as are speed limits anywhere else. Dogs are not admitted to Spurn at all.

Spurn Head is a thread of land flung out into the mouth of the

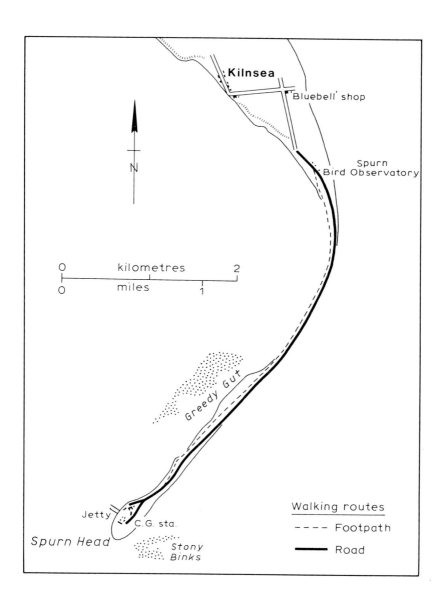

Kilnsea

Bluebell shop

Spurn
Bird Observatory

N

| kilometres | 2 |
| miles | 1 |

Greedy Gut

Jetty

Spurn Head

C.G. sta.

Stony
Binks

Walking routes

- - - - Footpath

———— Road

Humber Estuary by the North Sea, which ceaselessly gnaws at the boulder clay cliffs of the Holderness coast and carries eroded material southwards to deposit it at Spurn. This is only part of the story, however, for as the tides create Spurn so they also destroy it; building the southern tip ever further out into the estuary while scouring away at the peninsula behind until it collapses, first into a string of islands, then founders completely. At that, the process starts all over again, with another Spurn being built slightly to the west of the last one. No-one with even half an interest in countryside should either live in or visit the area without sharing the fascination of this purely temporary piece of the East Yorkshire and Derwent Area of the Ramblers' Association's patch.

The first time a headland at the mouth of the Humber enters the historical record is with the establishment of a monastery there in about AD 670. Even now, several spits later, it is impossible to imagine a better place for people seeking to contemplate the mutability of things. Either this spit or the next one to be formed gets a mention in an Icelandic Saga when a viking hero was wrecked on it, and a century later the remnants of Harold's army, fleeing defeat at Stamford Bridge in 1066, sailed from here. The next headland was a rather more civilised place, with its own town, a port which had a market, fair, chapel and, from 1303, Members of Parliament. A few decades later it had begun to be swept away and was gone by 1360. Now this thriving medieval port is just one of the list of settlements on the Holderness coast, still eroding fast, which have been lost to the sea.

The next spit to develop was the first to be called Spurn. A lighthouse was built here in 1427, perhaps the beginning of Spurn's long history of aids to navigation. But in about 1608 the sea took Spurn back once again and washed the remnants into the mouth of the Humber, forming an island which came to be called The Den. It has now been reduced to a muddy shoal which you will be able to see clearly at low tide. It is now known as Old Den and the channel between it and the present spit is the delightfully named Greedy Gut.

What we stand on today is the Spurn which developed after 1608. It is no more a permanent feature of the Humber Estuary than its predecessors. It has stood for rather longer, but only because of a series of ad hoc interventions attempting to stabilize it after it began to break up in the 1840s, when Parliament voted funds to fill in the breaches and construct the wooden groynes which can still be seen on the seaward side, reduced to skeletal sculptures by wind and waves.

However, it seems that the sands are literally running out on these attempts and that, if you want to see Spurn, you had better do it soon. The 1970s saw the onset of further serious erosion and major work was undertaken, strengthening the spit with rubble and laying down an immense bank of clay dug out from the underground North Sea Gas Terminal at nearby Easington. None of this has had much effect and the Spurn Bird Observatory's report for 1986 comments on the 'steady but relentless nature' of the erosion, accelerated by 'the surge tides of 3rd January 1976, 11th January 1978 and 1st February 1983'.

What you will see will not be some unspoilt stretch of countryside; in places it resembles nothing so much as a demolition site. But for all that it is a place which manages to be wild in spite of the numbers of people it attracts and romantic in the way which only places which have been through a lot of history can be.

When you arrive at the Bluebell, formerly a public house and now housing a small village shop, look up at a small plaque in the northern wall. It notes that when it was built in 1847 it stood 534 yards from the sea. It is about 100 yards from it now. Walk down the track leading east, past the caravan site, and you will see it rise up a bank. Nearby is a sign warning that the road is subject to erosion. This sign is clearly in the tradition of Great British Understatements, for beyond the bank the road simply runs out and the beach begins.

Turn back to the Bluebell and notice on your left what, at the time of writing, should qualify for a prize from someone as a clean and well-kept public convenience, with, miraculous to say, *hot* water for hand washing. Back at the Bluebell once more, turn left on the road after the house and head south towards Spurn Head, passing Southfield Farm. In a field just south of the farm are a series of concrete blocks. These are not the work of a local cubist-inspired Henry Moore, but our first intimation of the long association of Spurn Head with the paraphernalia and practice of war. This one is a tank trap and relic of the 1939-45 War, but Spurn's military history goes back to the Napoleonic wars, when batteries of guns were installed, just as they were in 1914-18 and 1939-45.

When you reach the gate of the nature reserve carry on along the road for a few yards until you reach a group of buildings, one of which is the Information and Sales Point. This is well worth a visit, for it has a display on the history of Spurn, its present wildlife and fossilised remains of that from long before, picked up from the beach. There is also a selection of books and souvenirs. Behind it is the Warren

81

Cottage, which is a good example of traditional Holderness architecture, built with cobbles washed out of the eroding cliffs. These were gathered from the beaches of Spurn and the cottage was built in the 1840's for a bailiff charged with collecting fees for this flourishing trade.

After the group of buildings turn off the road to the right on a track leading down to the salt flats of the Humber Estuary. Unless the tide is up, you can walk along the edge of the spit. In the nature of things this is going to be rather wet and boots would be an advantage. This is a wonderful area for watching the wading birds which feed here particularly from late July to April — Dunlin, Knot, Redshank, Turnstone, Curlews and Oystercatchers. Mallard and Shelduck feed on the estuary and Brent Geese winter there.

From here you can also look eastwards towards Hull and the high-tech towers of BP's chemical refinery at Saltend. To the south you can see the headland curving back into the Estuary with the lighthouse, now no longer used, near the tip. Echoing the lighthouse shape you will, unless the weather is too misty, be able to see the Dock Tower at Grimsby, on the other side of the Humber.

After about half a mile, leave the estuary shore and walk up onto the road. Here the headland is at its thinnest, a tightrope of road on a narrow ridge of sand between sea and estuary. The damage caused by erosion is very easy to see here. On the seaward side notice how rubble, much of it from demolished military installations, has been piled up to strengthen this fragile area known, for obvious reasons, as Narrow Neck. There is something slightly desolate about this part, but look around for the handsome blue-green Sea Holly. If you walk along the road for a little you will see, crossing it diagonally, of all incongruous things, what appear to be railway lines.

And that is just what they are, for a railway once ran the length of the peninsula. It was a military railway, built during the 1914-18 War to transport materials to the point, where guns were installed. The line was $3\frac{1}{4}$ miles long, and began at the village of Kilnsea. It had its own locomotives, but one of its chief sources of fascination for railway buffs is the use it made of sail power. Taking advantage of the windy situation of the exposed headland, a platelayers' bogie was fitted with a sail and goods and passengers regularly travelled by windpower. The sail was handled like that of a boat, but the bogie had no means of braking. As it reached speeds of 40 mph this meant that the usual substitutes, like throwing a sleeper onto the track before the front

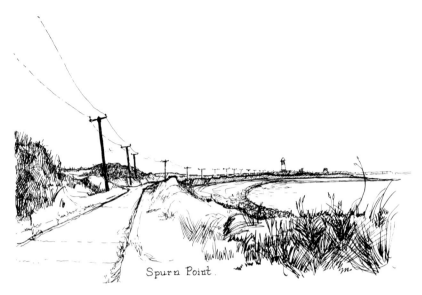

Spurn Point.

wheels, or jumping off before the end of the line, must have been somewhat hazardous.

Beyond Narrow Neck the headland widens out and the sand dunes become higher. This is a good area to look out for typical seashore and sand-dune plants. Marram grass, without which the dunes would blow away, is common, as is the Sea Buckthorn, a handsome and uncommon shrub ablaze in autumn with bright orange berries. These make it particularly important as a source of food for migrating birds. A phenomenon of the spring is the Spring Beauty, a delicate little white flower apparently floating in a green leafy cup.

The best walking from here to the point is the beach, a good hunting ground for fossils. In any case there is no access by land to the 'business end' of Spurn. Here are concentrated a base for the Humber pilots who guide ships up the treacherous Humber estuary, a coastguard station and lifeboat station with a resident crew. From 1893 until 1946 there was a tiny school for the children of the lifeboatmen and the service personnel who lived here a life of isolation, almost totally surrounded by the sea. A booklet about the school called *The School at Spurn Point* by Larry Malkin, Ann Stothard and Dorothy Smith contains a fascinating selection of excerpts from the school Log Book. Reports mention the children being rather backward owing to 'the peculiar and remote situation of this little school', but the 'object' lessons they had on the migrating birds, the dead seal which they were allowed to examine before it was buried, the special lessons on the sailing ships they saw going up the Humber, must have taught them much not available to children in more conventional settings.

From the point, if you are lucky enough to be there at the right stage of the tide, you can see the ships waiting for Humber Pilots just off the mouth of the estuary, and the pilot cutter leave the jetty to weave about among them in a flurry of bow-wave and wash. Then the big ships set off to the ports which line the estuary and rivers further inland. This is as far as Spurn point has progressed so far, though more material from the vanishing cliffs of Holderness can be seen piled up in the shoal just to the seaward of the point, known as Stony Binks. And it is as far as you can go, though the journey back is just as fascinating and there is much more to see, hear and find out. You may find that the six miles to the point and back take much longer than you thought they would, with so many opportunities and temptations to 'stand and stare'.

Ann Holt